**Nuclear Power
and
Legal Advocacy**

Nuclear Power and Legal Advocacy

The Environmentalists and the Courts

Constance Ewing Cook
Albion College

LexingtonBooks
D.C. Heath and Company
Lexington, Massachusetts
Toronto

Library of Congress Cataloging in Publication Data

Cook, Constance Ewing
    Nuclear power and legal advocacy.

    Bibliography: p.
    Includes index.
    1. Atomic power—Law and legislation—United States. 2. United
States. Nuclear Regulatory Commission. 3. Judicial review of administra-
tive acts—United States. 4. Pressure groups—United States. I. Title.
KF2138.C66   343'.73'092   79-3277
ISBN 0-669-03441-x

Copyright © 1980 by D.C. Heath and Company

Second printing, June 1981

Published simultaneously in Canada

Printed in the United States of America

International Standard Book Number: 0-669-03441-x

Library of Congress Catalog Card Number: 79-3277

For my children,
Jay and Amy Cook

Contents

Acknowledgments

This study is based largely on research done as part of my doctoral program at Boston University while I was living in Michigan. In the course of my research, I placed heavy reliance on the resources and personnel of both the University of Michigan, especially the Law School, and Consumers Power Company, where my work was not only tolerated but also facilitated.

I especially want to thank my two advisers at Boston University, Professors Betty Zisk and John Fletcher in the Political Science Department, for their perceptive and constructive criticism. I also profited from their logistical help in the course of this long–distance academic project. In addition, I am grateful to Professor Jeffrey Berry of Tufts University for his advice and encouragement, as well as to all those who gave generously of their time for my interviews.

Finally, a major share of the credit for this research goes to my husband, Jim. It was he who initially stimulated my interest in the nuclear power controversy and then shared his technical training and familiarity with the problems of utilities. Besides serving as a source of data and advice, he offered me moral support, enthusiastically and without equivocation. However, neither he nor the others to whom I am indebted necessarily agree with all my interpretations and conclusions.

Introduction

The accident at the Three Mile Island atomic plant in the spring of 1979 may have dealt the fatal blow to further development of commercial nuclear power in the United States. In any case, the subsequent protest march by 100,000 people in Washington, D.C., on May 6, 1979, convinced anyone who was still uncertain that public opposition to atomic energy was very widespread. The antinuclear movement had become national in its scope, incorporating a growing segment of the American public. The political obstacles to further development of nuclear plants were enormous, and there were also real doubts as to whether the existing seventy–one reactors in the United States would be allowed to continue to generate the 13 percent of the nation's electric energy for which they were then responsible.

Why did a nuclear accident that did not immediately cause a single injury or fatality suddenly activate such a massive response? Had public opinion become antinuclear overnight? Why were governmental institutions so amenable to pleas for antinuclear policymaking? How firm was the nation's commitment to atomic energy?

The answer is that, unbeknownst to much of the general population, the development of new commercial nuclear power plants had stopped more than two years earlier in 1977. A major nuclear trade publication proclaimed in November, 1977, "In the opinion of many, the giant United States nuclear industry is slowly, very slowly, bleeding to death."[1] Environmentalists concurred with the industry's evaluation of its own plight at that time. Anthony Roisman, a prominent antinuclear lawyer, concluded, "People looking back will say 1977 was when the United States decided to abandon nuclear power . . ."[2] The Union of Concerned Scientists also announced in 1977 that nuclear power was dead, and the antinuclear group could turn its energies to other topics.[3] Similarly, the Nader organization and many other environmental groups decided in 1977 to work on phasing out the existing atomic plants because nuclear power expansion no longer seemed likely and worthy of the groups' concern.[4]

Those portrayals of the nuclear industry's demise in 1977 reflect the realities of the new plant construction prognosis. While 126 new atomic reactors had been ordered by utilities in the nuclear power boom years from 1971–1974,[5] the order for the Carroll County plant in Illinois was the only authentic nuclear plant order placed by any utility in the country during all of 1977 and 1978.[6] Furthermore, it appeared that there would be no new orders placed in 1979 either. Although the Atomic Energy Commission had forecast in 1972 that there would probably be at least 150 nuclear power reactors operating in the United States by 1980, that prediction was not to be fulfilled. It appeared that by 1980 there would actually be only half the number of units forecast in 1972.

Thus, it is evident that nuclear power development had been largely curtailed long before the Three Mile Island accident. The explanations for that curtailment are both numerous and complex; and although decisions regarding the development of atomic energy were once considered to be technical and economic in nature, the reasons for its demise are largely political. Like most questions of public policy, the nuclear controversy can be conceptualized as an interest group struggle. The interest groups that support and oppose nuclear power, the nuclear industry on the one hand and the antinuclear environmental groups on the other, have confronted each other in a variety of policymaking institutions: Congress, the Executive branch, state and local governments, and, as examined here, the Nuclear Regulatory Commission and the courts. Nuclear power policymaking in each of these arenas should be clearly understood because the outcome of the controversy over atomic energy will have a significant effect on the country's future energy supply and way of life.

This book explicates the regulatory and judicial policymaking processes regarding nuclear power. In so doing, it especially examines the use and impact of legal advocacy. Legal advocacy, as used here, refers to the interest group strategy of filing suits to initiate judicial involvement in the nuclear power controversy. The lawsuits ordinarily deal with issues on which the regulatory agency has already made its rulings. The judiciary provides an especially informative vehicle for the examination of the controversy because it is the most passive of our policymaking institutions. Courts cannot solicit their own policy agenda and must wait for cases to appear on the docket before becoming involved in policy issues. The study of legal advocacy thereby focuses attention not only on judicial policymaking but also on regulatory rulings and on the interest groups that initiate and become parties to the litigation. As Justice Felix Frankfurter once observed, "The Court is a good mirror, an excellent mirror, of which historians for some reason have little availed themselves, of the struggles of dominant forces outside the Court."[7]

There are three interrelated objectives for this research. The first goal is a comparative analysis of the antinuclear environmental groups and the nuclear industry. The relative capabilities of public interest groups, in this case the environmentalists, will be contrasted with those of private interest groups, here represented by the established, traditional businesses that comprise the nuclear industry. Public interest groups are often depicted as political underdogs, struggling against great odds with the titans of industry to influence governmental policymaking. Conventional wisdom holds that big business enters the political arena with extensive organizational expertise and the economic resources to implement effective political strategies. Public interest groups, on the other hand, are conceptualized as ad hoc organizations made up of political novices operating on a shoestring budget. All those assumptions will be examined here by comparing the two sets of interest groups with regard to their organizational frameworks (including ideological motivations, communications networks, and cohesion) as well as their resources (including funds, leadership skills, coalitions with other groups, and legal expertise).

The second research objective is a determination of the political strategy used by each interest group and the reasons for its choice of strategy in the course of atomic energy litigation. Before most lawsuits involving nuclear power issues can be filed, rulings on the issues under contention must be made by the Nuclear Regulatory Commission (formerly the Atomic Energy Commission) which is the independent regulatory agency with statutory responsibility for setting nuclear plant standards and also licensing the plants. The Commission is, thus, a quasi-judicial body itself; and its rulings represent the first phase in the judicial policymaking process. The interest group's choice of strategy and its inclination to use legal advocacy and appeal the Commission's decisions to the courts are largely dependent upon its relationship with the Commission.

Conventional wisdom holds that the close relationship which a regulatory agency has with its clientele industry, that is, the regulated industry, gives that industry an advantageous position with regard to influencing bureaucratic policy decisions. Consequently, public interest group intervenors question the effectiveness of their participation in regulatory hearings, especially with regard to technical issues, and tend to believe that the content of policy decisions is predetermined. In order to examine that belief, the relationships of both sets of interest groups with the Commission will be described, and their relative influence on Commission procedures will be analyzed. Does the existence of a regulatory agency and complex regulatory requirements for a high-risk technology give public interest groups any real potential impact on bureaucratic policymaking? How are interest group political strategies affected by the groups' relationships with the Commission? Is legal advocacy likely to be used by both sets of interest groups to appeal administrative rulings to the courts?

The third research goal for this study is an analysis of the role of the judiciary in the nuclear power controversy. As Commission rulings are appealed to the courts for judicial review, the characteristics of the judicial process are as important as the nature of the court opinions. Therefore, an assessment will be made not only of the judicial policy output but also of the impact of the judicial process on the interest group litigants. What have been the major judicial rulings regarding nuclear power litigation? Has the judiciary itself been an active policymaking institution, or has it upheld previous Commission rulings? Does the group that wins its case in court gain the greatest advantage from the litigation process, as one would expect? Is legal advocacy a useful interest group strategy? In short, what impact has the judicial process had on the development of nuclear power?

The subject matter of this study addresses itself to a number of gaps in the existing political science literature. Unfortunately, in the last ten to fifteen years, interest group studies have been unfashionable and infrequently undertaken. The interest group theory first formulated by Arthur Bentley[8] and then further developed in David Truman's *The Governmental Process*[9] requires normative and empirical supplementation. Especially at the end of the 1970s, there seems to be a clear need for a resurgence of scholarly concern with interest groups. As the importance of political parties in American politics has undergone a decline, interest groups have been supplanting the two parties as the major informal political units influencing national policymaking. Therefore, it is now particularly important to understand the characteristics and tactics of interest groups and their contributions to national policymaking.

In the past there have rarely been systematic comparisons of both sides in an interest group controversy. The few existing works include: Bauer, Pool, and Dexter's *American Business and Public Policy;*[10] Schattschneider's *Politics, Pressures and Tariff;*[11] and Bailey's *Congress Makes a Law.*[12] In addition, the phenomenon of the last decade involving the development of public interest groups has elsewhere received inadequate scholarly treatment. Although the members of public interest groups have themselves written a great deal about their organizations, there are few objective analyses of these new interest groups. Among the few are Berry's *Lobbying for the People*[13] and Vogle's "Promoting Pluralism: The Public Interest Movement and the American Reform Tradition."[14]

Just as interest groups have received little heuristic attention, so legal advocacy as an interest group strategy has been infrequently described. The few good expository studies of legal advocacy include: Orren's "Standing to Sue: Interest Group Conflict in the Federal Courts";[15] Peltason's *Federal Courts in the Political Process;*[16] Sax's *Defending the Environment;*[17] and Vose's "Litigation As a Form of Pressure Group Activity."[18] Furthermore, there have rarely been analyses of the use of legal advocacy by opposing interest groups in a single controversy and the effect of their tactics on the judicial policymaking process. Vose's *Caucasians Only: The Supreme Court, the NAACP, and the Restrictive Covenant Cases*[19] is one of the few such works and is referred to here as the model for the appraisal of potential interest group influence on the judiciary.

In regard to gaps in political science literature involving the judicial process, the major void has appeared in impact studies. Impact studies have concentrated primarily on compliance or noncompliance with judicial rulings,[20] and they have rarely been applied to the judicial review of administrative decision making, the regulation of industry, or to environmental cases generally, all of which are included here. Furthermore, there is a history of interest group utilization of legal advocacy simply for the purpose of generating delay, especially in regard to the implementation of regulatory rulings. The duration of the judicial process is sometimes more significant in determining the outcome of a policy conflict than is the nature of the court's ruling. There has been little examination of the impact of the lengthy judicial policymaking process on the resolution of national policy controversies, and it is intended that the attention given here to that phenomenon will supplement the existing public policy research.

The forthcoming material is organized into nine chapters. Chapter 1 gives a general description of the background of the nuclear power controversy, including the energy situation and the related economic conditions in the United States, as well as the extent of public and governmental support for nuclear power development. Chapter 2 surveys the national antinuclear environmental groups and the nuclear industry and compares them as to their organizational structures and resources, including the legal expertise available to them.

Chapter 3 concerns the Commission: the statutes that established it and the nature of its licensing process, as well as the statutes relevant to the judicial review of its decision making. The relationships of the environmental groups and the nuclear industry with the Commission are examined in order to explain their inclinations to use or avoid the use of legal advocacy.

Since the inception of commercial nuclear power, antinuclear groups have petitioned for court review of hundreds of licensing and regulatory decisions made by the Commission. Chapter 4 surveys the major judicial opinions handed down in nuclear power litigation and also makes an initial assessment of their effect on the nuclear industry.

In order to illustrate the use and impact of the judicial review process, the controversy surrounding the construction of a nuclear plant in Midland, Michigan, is used as a representative case study. Midland differs from other nuclear plant controversies primarily in that it presents an extreme version of what has occurred so often elsewhere in somewhat modified form. Chapter 5 surveys the prelude to litigation at Midland: the political mobilization of the environmental groups and the nuclear industry (according to the interest group organizational framework used for their national counterparts in chapter 2) and the results of the Commission's licensing process for the Midland plant's construction.

When the environmental groups appealed the Commission's issuance of a construction permit for the Midland plant, the United States Court of Appeals for the District of Columbia Circuit remanded the permit to the Commission for further hearings.[21] Chapter 6 explains the reasons for the court's ruling. It also investigates the potential interest group influences on the court in order to determine the extent of the groups' involvement in the judicial policymaking process. Chapter 7 describes the Supreme Court's review of the lower court's ruling and its sharp rebuke of the Court of Appeals in the Midland case,[22] again examining the potential influences on the Court as well as the opinion itself.

Chapter 8 surveys the effect of the Supreme Court ruling on the interest groups at Midland, showing how the impact of the regulatory and judicial process is a deterrent to the development of nuclear power. Chapter 9 consists of a summary of the research conclusions and an appraisal of the future of legal advocacy in the nuclear controversy. The chapter ends with the judgment that, regardless of future events, the use of legal advocacy has already been an effective strategy for the public interest groups and has contributed to the decline of the nuclear industry.

Nuclear Power
and
Legal Advocacy

1

The Economic and Political Background

Economics and Energy

The American public began to utilize electric power in the early part of the twentieth century, and there has been an annual increase in electricity usage ever since. Historically, energy, and especially electric energy, has mechanized society, replacing human labor with machinery. Electricity is the most sophisticated form of energy, and the American standard of living has been heavily dependent upon it for home appliances, lighting, major industrial machines, and mass communications.

As the American demand for energy started to grow, there appeared to be an inexhaustible supply of it. Electricity became increasingly affordable, with its price declining as technological improvements and economies of scale accompanied the development of widespread electrification. Declining prices contributed to the increase in demand; and, from 1960 to 1973, for example, there was an average annual growth rate of about 7 percent in the American public's consumption of electricity. In addition, this was generally a period of economic expansion caused, in part, by the Vietnam war. The development of commercial nuclear power coincided with this period of nonnuclear electric power expansion and economic optimism.

The history of nuclear power dates back to 1942 when controlled nuclear fission was first achieved as a result of the Manhattan Project, the government's weapons research program during World War II. Weapons-grade uranium (U_{235}) was obtained from uranium isotope separation facilities to produce the first atomic bombs, and then nuclear reactors were developed by the military to provide plutonium for additional bombs. Later, a different type of reactor was used to power submarines and surface ships, particularly aircraft carriers.

In 1946, the Atomic Energy Act was enacted by Congress. It created the Atomic Energy Commission (AEC), an agency with the dual purpose of promoting the development of atomic energy for national security and also controlling it to safeguard public health and safety. In 1954, the nation committed itself to the nonmilitary use of atomic power through endorsement of the Atoms for Peace proposal. It was embodied in the 1954 amendments to the Atomic Energy Act which authorized and encouraged the development of nuclear power by private industry. By way of demonstration and encouragement, the government used a naval reactor design to

1

build a nuclear power plant which began operation in Shippingport, Pennsylvania, in 1957. Then, in 1959, the first private nuclear generating plant went into operation in Dresden, Illinois.

Nuclear power initially appeared to offer an abundant supply of clean energy that would be relatively inexpensive. It was expected that the low cost of uranium fuel would more than offset the large capital costs of building atomic plants. Consequently, after a period of demonstration, technical improvement, and reduction in costs, the commercialization of nuclear power appeared to be well on its way. By the latter part of the 1960s, electric utilities were ordering and building atomic plants in increasing numbers.

However, at about the same time, the average cost of all forms of electricity had begun to rise. The factors that had contributed to the lowering of the cost of electricity during its developmental period were eventually overtaken by inflation. Nevertheless, the combination of the expanding American economy and the United States involvement in Vietnam meant that the demand for electricity did not immediately decline as its real price went up. An inflationary spiral was in motion.

Then, in October, 1973, the Organization of Petroleum Exporting Countries (OPEC) initiated an embargo on oil delivery to the United States in retaliation for American political support for Israel. When the embargo was lifted after a two-month period, oil prices increased. In fact, the cost of oil quadrupled between 1973 and 1975 and then continued its steady climb, meanwhile pulling up the cost of other fuels with it. Since the American economy was already strained anyway, the oil problems triggered a major recession in 1974 and 1975 with interest rates at record levels. As the country emerged from its recession, the cost of all forms of energy remained high, and there continued to be a significant rate of inflation.

Starting almost immediately with the oil embargo, Americans began to realize that the era when energy seemed both inexhaustible and inexpensive had come to an end. The government promoted cost-effective conservation programs to avoid unnecessary waste of energy, and both industrial and individual electric customers began to implement these measures. The conservation programs combined with the reduction in economic activity during the recession to produce a sudden decrease in the demand for electricity. In fact, the annual growth rate of production of electricity dropped to an unprecedented low of 0.55 percent from 1973 to 1974, followed by 2.74 percent from 1974 to 1975.[1] Therefore, the utilities experienced an abrupt reduction in their revenues. This reduction in revenues occurred while the utilities were in the midst of major new plant construction programs. Construction decisions had been made when the rate of increase in the production of electricity had averaged 6.62 percent from 1970 to 1973[2] and even higher in the previous decade. Furthermore, the high interest rates increased the cost of borrowing money to finance the construction programs. The utilities, caught in this dilemma, were forced to cancel or postpone as many power plant projects as possible.

Throughout the 1970s, economic, technical, and political complications had been arising in regard to the procurement and usage of all forms of fuel for electric power generation. The United States wanted to avoid excessive dependence on foreign oil since its supply and price could not be controlled, and the oil imports were contributing to balance of payments deficits and domestic inflation. In regard to American natural gas, there had been supply problems since the early 1970s, and environmental concerns arose in regard to coal and, especially, nuclear power.

Nonetheless, the annual increase in American usage of electricity continued after 1973, though at a slower pace. Since the average annual electricity generation growth rate was 3.56 percent from 1973 to 1977,[3] additional electric power plants were built to meet the demand. As more nuclear plants went into operation, the percentage of electricity supplied by nuclear power in the United States, which was less than 5 percent in 1973, expanded to nearly 13 percent by 1978. However, as the country's usage of atomic energy was increasing, political support for continued development of nuclear plants was eroding.

Politics and Energy

The political climate for the development of nuclear power initially had been very favorable, as reflected in the commitments of the various Presidents to that form of energy. It was President Eisenhower who, shortly after taking office in 1953, suggested the Atoms-for-Peace program leading to the commercial development of nuclear power. Similar support for private nuclear power was given unequivocally by succeeding administrations. When the 1974 oil embargo led Americans to consider achieving energy independence, President Richard Nixon proposed that nuclear power become the source, eventually, of over half the nation's electricity.

It was not until about the time that President Gerald Ford took office in 1974 that the atomic energy issue became truly politicized. Ford enthusiastically endorsed the pronuclear position, calling for faster licensing procedures to expedite the development of atomic power plants and suggesting greater dependence on nuclear power in this country and abroad. Ford's State of the Union Address in 1975 asked for 200 more nuclear power reactors by 1985.

Although he had had training as a nuclear engineer, candidate Jimmy Carter campaigned on a platform that was markedly less supportive of nuclear power than his opponent Gerald Ford in the 1976 election. Carter's policy statement on "Nuclear Energy and World Order" said, "U.S.

dependence on nuclear power should be kept to the minimum necessary to meet our needs. We should apply much stronger safety standards as we regulate its use."[4] Then, following his election, Carter appointed several environmentalists to sensitive positions in major agencies, such as the Council on Environmental Quality and the Environmental Protection Agency. When Carter made James Schlesinger his head of the newly created Department of Energy, Schlesinger disavowed personal advocacy of nuclear power in spite of his background as a former chairman of the Atomic Energy Commission.[5]

Although President Carter took a strong stand against the Clinch River Breeder Reactor and reprocessing because of his views on weapons proliferation, he did not cut off support for nuclear power entirely. His much publicized energy plan announced on April 20, 1977, advocated further development of the light water nuclear reactor, but it recommended stricter safety and inspection standards. Accordingly, the Carter administration proposed a Nuclear Licensing Reform Bill in 1978 which included provisions for standardized nuclear plants, intervenor funding, quicker licensing procedures, state control over environmental and energy demand decisions, and some changes in the format of regulatory hearings. Neither the proponents nor the opponents of nuclear power supported the bill since it contained provisions inimical to both. Consequently, the bill died in Congressional committee in 1978, and Carter intended to reintroduce it in 1979 prior to the Three Mile Island accident. However, that occurrence precluded immediate resubmission of the bill.

Thus, although President Carter was unwilling to prohibit nuclear power altogether, his endorsement of it fell far short of the complete support it had received from previous administrations. Essentially, Carter's position was an ambivalent one, and he did not provide the nuclear industry with the political support it needed for further development of atomic plants. Nor did Carter please the environmentalists: in the wake of Three Mile Island, they charged that Carter had deceived them by his failure to phase out nuclear plants altogether. The President countered, however, that an immediate shutdown of all atomic plants was "out of the question."[6] With both the nuclear industry and the environmentalists dissatisfied with Carter's position regarding atomic energy, there was no doubt that the issue would play a prominent part in the 1980 Presidential campaign.

In the last decade, there has been significant erosion not only in Presidential support for atomic energy development but also in Congressional support for it. In 1954, when Congress amended the Atomic Energy Act, it established the Joint Committee on Atomic Energy (JCAE). It was composed of nine Representatives and nine Senators chosen by the Congressional leaders. In order to avoid House and Senate conflicts and to capitalize on the committee's expertise in technical matters, the JCAE was initially given authority as the only joint committee able to sponsor legislation itself.

Similarly, all nuclear-related matters were considered to be under its jurisdiction, and its members were usually strong supporters of atomic energy development. As a result, it was charged that the JCAE was "established as a watchdog of the AEC, [but] underwent a transformation from a healthy adversary to the AEC's leading apologist, protector and partner."[7]

In 1974, Congress began to redistribute the JCAE oversight responsibilities. Then, in 1977, the 95th Congress dissolved the JCAE altogether and dispersed its legislative authority over commercial nuclear power among a variety of committees in the House of Representatives: Interior and Insular Affairs, Government Operations, Appropriations, Interstate and Foreign Commerce, and Science and Technology. In the Senate, the committees given some jurisdiction over nuclear matters included Energy and Natural Resources, Environment and Public Works, Governmental Affairs, Appropriations, Labor and Human Relations, and Commerce, Science, and Transportation. In addition, questions regarding nuclear weaponry and proliferation were to come before the Armed Services and International Relations Committees in the House and the Armed Services and Foreign Relations Committees in the Senate. In each House, many of the numerous standing committees dealing with nuclear-related matters also had more than one subcommittee with jurisdiction over atomic energy issues. The result, of course, was increased involvement by many legislators in the Congressional atomic energy policymaking process.

Along with the Congressional committee changes came reorganization of the bureaucratic organizations controlling nuclear power. In 1974, Congress abolished the Atomic Energy Commission (AEC) in response to public criticism regarding its "schizophrenic mandate to promote as well as regulate nuclear power."[8] With the Energy Reorganization Act, Congress replaced the AEC with two separate agencies: the Energy Research and Development Administration (ERDA) which would recommend energy budgetary priorities and assume responsibility for energy research and demonstration programs, and the Nuclear Regulatory Commission (NRC) which would regulate nuclear power plants.

In the last decade or so, Congress has been faced with many other questions involving nuclear power in addition to these administrative reorganizations. Some of the Congressional decisions have been supportive of the nuclear industry, such as the renewal of the Price-Anderson Act (limited liability nuclear insurance) in 1975 and the funding for the Clinch River Breeder Reactor in 1977 and 1978. Furthermore, the National Environmental Policy Act (NEPA), the statute that has thus far caused the greatest dislocation in the process of licensing atomic power plants, was not intended to be specifically antinuclear. Its enactment in 1969 was not a matter that excited much interest in Congress or aroused strong emotions at the time. The bill's language was vague, and Congress did little to determine its potential consequences. Therefore, NEPA was able to pass in the Senate without debate, and the significant provision that requires environmental impact statements for "major Federal action" was not even included in the bill that originally passed the House. However, the courts interpreted NEPA in such a way that the Commission was obliged to restructure and augment its licensing process for atomic power plants. The result was a substantial increase in the complexity of the regulatory and licensing process, as well as frequent appeals for judicial review of the Commission's rulings.

Although the passage of NEPA was not indicative of antinuclear sentiment in Congress, there has since been a gradual increase in Congressional skepticism regarding the merits of nuclear power development. As a result, there has been more support for passage of an intervenor financing bill which would authorize the Nuclear Regulatory Commission to reimburse private citizens and public interest groups for their participation in licensing and rulemaking hearings. A large number of other bills have been introduced in the wake of Three Mile Island that also reflect an increase in Congressional concern about nuclear plant safety. Some of the bills mandate new procedures for dealing with nuclear plant accidents; others suggest a moratorium on nuclear plant licensing and/or new regulations for existing plants; and others are intended to phase out nuclear power altogether.

The politicization of the nuclear power issue and erosion of legislative support has been even more significant in some states and localities than in Congress. Although the Atomic Energy Act gave the federal government full jurisdiction over the regulation of nuclear power for the protection of public health and safety, many states have in recent years sought to control nuclear development within their borders through restrictions on plant siting or through regulation of rate structures and pollution control. In 1977, seven states passed laws prohibiting high-level waste disposal; and especially restrictive legislation regarding atomic power plants has been enacted in California, Maine, and Oregon. Antinuclear statutes, particularly with regard to transportation ordinances, have also been adopted by some individual towns and counties, especially in New England.

However, until recently, the majority of the public have been supportive of nuclear power development when given the opportunity to vote on the issue. In 1976, 20 percent of the nation's population was exposed to state initiatives on atomic energy. None of these represented actual bans on nuclear power but, rather, were safeguards proposals that would make nuclear development subject to state legislative approval. That approval, in turn, was contingent upon the enactment of such policies as a satisfactory national plan to dispose of radioactive wastes, full insurance indemnity for nuclear accidents, and changes in plant operation standards, with the wording differing from state to state. The 1976 antinuclear referenda were voted down in California, Oregon, Ohio, Washington, Arizona, Colorado, and Montana.

Since 1976, there has been a gradual attrition in public support for nuclear power plants. When atomic energy referendum questions were presented to the voters of Hawaii and Montana in November, 1978, antinuclear victories resulted in both states. Furthermore, public opinion polls have also indicated an increase in public concern regarding the safety of atomic plants, especially those being built in one's own geographical area. In fact, in a 1978 Edison Electric Institute survey, more people said they were against the construction of a nuclear plant in their own area than were for it. The change in public perception of nuclear plant safety is most striking when one compares the 1978 responses with 1971 figures. Fifty-seven percent of the public in 1971 said it would be "all right" to build a nuclear plant in their area, as compared to 25 percent "against it"; by 1978, only 41 percent favored the construction of a nuclear plant, and 43 percent opposed it.[9] The Three Mile Island accident further eroded public confidence in atomic plants.

Summary and Conclusions

Throughout the twentieth century, the United States has experienced an annual increase in the usage of electricity. As the price of electricity initially declined, the American standard of living became more and more dependent on electric power. However, by the late 1960s, the costs of all fuels and generating facilities were on the rise, and further increases in the price of electricity were triggered by the 1973 oil embargo and subsequent economic dislocations. Although the higher costs of electricity have encouraged conservation, the overall increase in the American demand for electric power has continued, though at a slower rate of growth.

Since the beginning of its commercial development in the late 1950s, atomic energy has supplied a growing percentage of the country's electric power, generating nearly 13 percent of the nation's electricity in 1978. However, paradoxically, political support for the continued development of nuclear power has been eroding. Jimmy Carter is the first American President who has not given his unequivocal endorsement to commercial atomic energy; and Congressional committee changes, administrative reorganizations, and voting patterns have shown increasing opposition to nuclear power and politicization of the issue. In addition, antinuclear statutes and referenda have been passed in some states and localities, reflecting the fact that the majority of people no longer favor the construction of a nuclear plant in their own geographic area. Not surprisingly, the Three Mile Island nuclear plant accident has further intensified concern about atomic plant safety. It remains, therefore, to account for this sharp decline in governmental and public support for atomic energy.

2 The Interest Groups: Organizations and Resources

The decline in the pace of development of nuclear power in the United States may be attributed to a variety of causes. One of these is the effective opposition of the antinuclear environmental groups to that source of energy. The environmental groups are public interest groups, and there is a popular belief that these groups are no match in the political arena for big business, here exemplified by the nuclear industry. Therefore, this chapter will compare the two sets of interest groups in the nuclear controversy and assess their relative capability to influence the nation's policymaking.

David Truman, in examining interest groups, hypothesized that a major factor determining the success of a group in achieving "access to the institutions of government" is the "degree and appropriateness of the group's organization."[1] As a prelude to the detailed examination of interest group access to and use of the judiciary for nuclear power policymaking, this chapter will examine and contrast the interest groups in regard to the degree and appropriateness of their organizations, that is, ideological motivations, organizational frameworks, communications networks, and cohesion, as well as their organizational resources which include funds, leadership skills, and coalitions with other groups. In addition, the organizations and resources available to each interest group for the use of litigation will be described and compared.

The Antinuclear Environmental Groups

Sheldon Novick's comment that "the fight over nuclear power is not an orderly engagement between well-organized forces. . . . "[2] is particularly applicable to the environmental groups that oppose nuclear power. The antinuclear forces are comprised of "citizen groups" or "public interest groups," terms which may be defined in a number of ways. Jeffrey M. Berry calls a "public interest group" one that "seeks a collective good, the achievement of which will not selectively and materially benefit the membership or activists of the organization."[3] Its organizational incentives are "purposive" or ideological in nature.[4] Peter Schuck uses a somewhat more restrictive definition of a public interest group, saying that it is "organized around a status or role which virtually all persons in the community are thought to share in common—the status of consumer, citizen, taxpayer,

9

member of the biosphere. . . . "[5] The antinuclear environmental organizations fit neatly into either Berry or Schuck's concepts of public interest groups.

The antinuclear groups at first glance seem to be motivated especially by their concern with safety issues. Consequently, they are posing a multitude of technical questions regarding the safety of the development of atomic energy. Underlying those questions, however, is a fundamental commitment on the part of many environmental groups to abolish nuclear power altogether. Three attitudes seem to reinforce this commitment. First, there is a basic pessimism about technology among many opponents of atomic energy. As Bupp and Derian commented, "To many in Western society, science and technology are now identified with deterioration in the quality of life."[6] Because nuclear power is linked in the public mind with atomic weaponry, it has become a symbol of the destructive potential of modern technology. Consequently, opposition to further development of nuclear power has come from these environmentalists who do not share the value structure of a scientifically oriented society and do not like "balancing risks against benefits."[7] The debate over the level of the minimum acceptable risk, therefore, obscures the objective of many environmentalists of applying a "zero-risk" standard to nuclear power technology.[8]

A second pervasive attitude underlying antinuclear sentiment is the dislike of industrial expansion: the no-growth or zero-growth concept, which would, in the amount of energy consumed, maintain the status quo. Many environmentalists favor "soft energy" sources, especially solar power, as a replacement for existing quantities of atomic power, and they believe that effective conservation measures could cut back energy usage to the point where nuclear power's loss would not be missed.

The third and related antinuclear group motivation is the concern about high degrees of economic centralization, with the expansion of the business establishment leading to a greater gap between rich and poor. The father of the economic decentralization concept is E.F. Schumacher, the British economist whose book *Small Is Beautiful* espouses antinuclear sentiments along with his preference for alternative technologies.[9] Ralph Nader explains his own opposition to nuclear power by first saying that it will "lead to more concentrated political and economic power in a few hands than another form of energy. . . [and] requires highly centralized institutions."[10] Because the construction of a nuclear power plant requires a huge capital investment, Nader feels that atomic energy and big business are intertwined. Thus, an antibusiness orientation is intermingled with the other antinuclear motivations.

Environmentalists' concern with thermal pollution originally served as the catalyst for the antinuclear movement. Environmental groups discovered in the 1960s that the heat discharged from the cooling system of nuclear plants would do more to upset the balance of the ecosystem in lakes and rivers and along the seacoast than the discharges from other types of power plants. This concern with thermal pollution led to the groups' involvement in the nuclear regulatory process which, in turn, caused skepticism about the general safety of atomic power. By Earth Day, 1970, an antinuclear feeling was part of some of the environmentalists' perspective.

The antinuclear movement is somewhat amorphous, and there are more groups involved than could possibly be named. The majority of these groups are local in nature, small in size, and often have formed in order to oppose one specific nuclear plant in their own area. They have no official membership list or by-laws since their organization is strictly ad hoc and fluid. Many of these small groups have been coordinated with other local groups in loose federations, such as the Clamshell Alliance. According to one study, there are probably about 20,000 voluntary environmental organizations in the United States,[11] and many of them oppose further development of nuclear power.

It was not until about 1973 that big names in public interest circles, such as the Nader organization and the Sierra Club, joined the opposition to nuclear power.[12] The Sierra Club has about fifty chapters across the United States, including Hawaii and Alaska. The extent of its opposition to nuclear power has varied.

The Nader organization is probably the largest and best-known opponent of atomic energy. Its antinuclear activities are coordinated by Critical Mass. Critical Mass helped with the antinuclear state referenda, advises groups on initiating state and local legislation to curb nuclear power, acts as a clearinghouse for existing and pending statutes, publishes a monthly newsletter on citizen efforts to stop atomic energy and has held national citizens' conferences to exchange antinuclear information. Critical Mass is affiliated with 175 local citizen groups. Another Nader-sponsored organization, now autonomous from the Nader group, is the Public Interest Research Group (PIRG). PIRG is a student-based group held together by a professional staff and represented in about twenty states, as well as at the local and regional levels. Its public interest work focuses on consumer issues of which its antinuclear lobbying is one offshoot.

Another organization which is actively involved in the battle against nuclear power is the Union of Concerned Scientists (UCS) which includes scientists and engineers among its members. It was formed in 1969, and its most significant contribution to the antinuclear movement has been the exposure of dissension within the scientific community on safety issues by gathering signatures from its members on reports that are critical of government regulatory policy and then publicizing these reports in the media. For example, on August 6, 1975, the UCS sent an antinuclear statement to Congress with 2300 signatures.[13]

Antinuclear environmental organizations, because of their noncommercial interests, are somewhat heterogeneous in membership. However, they typically draw much of their membership from the white–collar, middle class, educated segment of the population,[14] as well as from the affluent upper class.[15] In addition, the environmental groups, and the antinuclear groups in particular, rely heavily on large numbers of students and young people. Because the antinuclear organizations have a variety of concerns, there are sometimes differences of opinion within them regarding resource commitments and policies. However, these intra– or interorganizational disagreements do not deter them from their basic commitment to the crusade against atomic energy.

As Bernard Cohen has pointed out, heterogeneous interest groups, such as the antinuclear environmental forces, tend to spend much of their time educating and communicating with their members, as well as with the general public.[16] The distinction between communications with members and with the public in general is, therefore, blurred. Consequently, the communications links within the environmental movement are far more numerous than those connecting the more homogeneous, tangible nuclear industry. It is these communications which have been responsible for coordinating the tactics of the many small, local antinuclear environmental groups in order to form federations and mobilize effective political action.

To name a few of the environmental organizations' communications, the Friends of the Earth publishes the newsletter *Not Man Apart;* the Environmental Action Foundation puts out the monthly publication *The Power Line* on electric utility issues and political activism; the Center for Science in the Public Interest has a publication entitled *People and Energy* on citizen activism regarding energy issues; the Audubon Society has a monthly magazine entitled *Audubon;* and periodicals such as *Environment* and *Environmental Affairs* provide general information on the environmental movement. Some of the larger groups, such as the Sierra Club, the Nader organization, and Friends of the Earth, publish books as well. Whether in book, magazine or newsletter form, most of these communications, when they deal with the atomic energy issue, encourage antinuclear political activism and serve as guides to previous, current, and potential forms of protest.

The environmental groups, like all public interest groups, vary greatly in financial resources. Furthermore, the size of their budgets does not necessarily mean that a large percentage of them is spent on political activism or antinuclear activity specifically. Among those with very healthy budgets is the National Audubon Society which had an income of more than $7 million in 1972.[17] Generally speaking, foundation support has been the single biggest factor in encouraging the development and activities of consumer and environmental groups, with about a third of them receiving at least half of their funds from foundations. For instance, the $75,000 that is now spent annually by the Environmental Action Foundation on its utility project comes from small foundations, as well as from individual members.[18] There are many small antinuclear groups, however, that operate on a shoestring, with the money coming from private gifts or from nominal membership dues. Fortunately for most public interest groups, their staff usually feels a personal commitment to the causes they champion and are willing to work for salaries lower than they would earn elsewhere.[19]

The funds that are available to antinuclear groups are often used to full advantage, thanks to the dedication of most environmental group leaders. In fact, effective leadership is the most significant organizational resource from which these groups benefit. The leaders of the environmental movement have been particularly good at utilizing all the political strategies, both traditional and nontraditional, potentially available to the groups, so that the antinuclear battle has been waged in a wide variety of arenas. Their tactics have included protests, demonstrations, civil disobedience, and other low-budget media events which compensate for the lack of more funding. A good example of one such media event was the release of balloons warning of radiation hazards at nuclear plant sites on the anniversary of the bombing of Hiroshima. A much more costly and significant media event, however, was the release in the spring of 1979 of a disaster movie called *The China Syndrome.* It starred antinuclear activists Jane Fonda and Jack Lemmon and effectively portrayed atomic energy as a very dangerous source of electricity and the nuclear industry as a business run by executives concerned only with the size of their profits.

Although there are many celebrities and elected officials who sympathize with the antinuclear cause, they are not the real leaders of the movement. Rather, the heads of the various environmental groups do the strategic decision making; and, like the leadership of other public interest groups, it is typically of an oligarchic, personalized nature.[20] The organizations are run by the so called "active minority" whether or not they have a mass membership. Some of the most noteworthy leaders of the antinuclear movement include Henry Kendall and Daniel Ford of the Union of Concerned Scientists, Barry Commoner of the Scientists' Institute for Public Information, and Amory Lovins of the British Friends of the Earth.

Ralph Nader, as the father of the consumer movement, is certainly the best-known spokesperson for the public interest groups; and since 1973, he has made a strong personal commitment to the complete elimination of nuclear power plants.[21] His weekly newspaper column and his coverage by the media have yielded much publicity for the antinuclear forces. Although Nader's prestige is less than it once was, Berry points out, "The fact that Nader will appear at a press conference makes the conference a recognized media event."[22]

Another Nader asset from which the environmental groups have benefited has been his organizational skill. He has helped to stimulate the formation of a national network of antinuclear forces and has been helpful in recommending effective tactics. His recent book, written with John Abbotts and called *The Menace of Atomic Energy,* is the most comprehensive antinuclear strategy textbook available. It tells how to influence congressional legislation and the votes of individual members of Congress, as well as state legislators, the means of effective protest and intervention before the Nuclear Regulatory Commission and state public utility commissions, and the times when antinuclear litigation is appropriate. In short, this antinuclear bible explains how to politicize the nuclear question and details the Nader position on the pros and cons of the different forms of antinuclear activism.

The leaders of the various antinuclear organizations have been quite effective in increasing their strength by building coalitions with other groups. As Berry has stated, "coalitions are extremely popular among public interest lobbies,"[23] and public interest groups can often count on each other for support. The consumer groups that fight utilities on rate increases have often been glad to lend their support to the antinuclear environmental groups. In addition, the nature of the antinuclear movement has especially attracted political activists of the 1960s, as at the Seabrook nuclear plant demonstration in May, 1977, when "the cadre that planned the occupation consisted mainly of veterans of the civil rights and anti-war movements."[24]

The antinuclear groups' readiness to form coalitions and the organizational expertise of their leadership were particularly demonstrated by the protest against atomic energy in Washington, D.C., on May 6, 1979. In the wake of the Three Mile Island accident, a new alliance of environmentalists and public interest groups formed for the purpose of mobilizing as large a protest group as possible. The result was a rally by an estimated 100,000 protestors, again reminiscent of the demonstrations against the Vietnam war.

The antinuclear organizations have repeatedly been more effective than the nuclear industry in mobilizing public support. Women have been particularly receptive to the environmentalists' appeals. In the California initiative campaign, for instance, the antinuclear groups' "workforce as well as their principal audience was women,"[25] and the League of Women Voters issued a statement that expressed opposition to further development of light water reactors in March, 1978. As for black organizations, Vernon Jordan, President of the National Urban League, has split from the NAACP on the nuclear issue and made a statement in January, 1978, expressing disapproval of atomic energy as an alternative source of energy. The environmentalists also found an ally in the National Council of Churches of Christ in the U.S.A. which adopted a well-publicized resolution on March 4, 1976, endorsing a moratorium on plutonium reprocessing and use of plutonium in breeder reactors.

Another resource at the disposal of the environmental groups has been legal expertise. Public interest groups in general, including the antinuclear groups, tend to be dominated by lawyers, thereby giving a "decidedly legalistic, litigation–oriented cast to public interest activity."[26] There are now appropriately 600 lawyers employed on a full–time basis by 100 public interest groups.[27]

Besides the lawyers who work for many of the environmental groups, there are a number of major public interest groups that emphasize legal work. Among these are the Natural Resources Defense Council (NRDC), the Environmental Defense Fund (EDF), Business and Professional People for the Public Interest (BPI), and the Center for Law and Social Policy. The activity of these public interest groups is limited to legal advocacy, and their support comes from their members and from the foundations. The Ford Foundation has been especially generous in its grants for public interest law, having provided millions of dollars of seed money to facilitate the establishment of the NRDC, the EDF, and the Center for Law and Social Policy in their early years.[28]

In addition to the public interest law firms, there are traditional law firms that provide legal services for environmental groups *pro bono,* meaning that it is done free of charge or at substantially reduced rates. Altogether there are now seventy-five public interest law centers.[29] One of these is the firm of Berlin, Roisman, and Kessler of which well–known antinuclear lawyer Anthony Roisman is a part. It does a variety of types of legal work so that it can earn enough to be able to provide public interest lawyers for the environmental groups free of charge.[30] It typically costs $100,000 for an antinuclear group to oppose an atomic energy plant through court action,[31] but the *pro bono* work and foundation support have often financed the litigation. Thus, many antinuclear groups have adequate organizational facilities and resources for the use of court action. As with all their other available resources, the environmental leaders have maximized the use of their legal expertise and funding as one of their many political strategies in the nuclear power controversy.

The Nuclear Industry

The term *nuclear industry,* as used here, refers to the companies that build, buy, or supply nuclear power plants. The electric power companies were originally encouraged by the Atomic Energy Commission to begin the commercial development of nuclear power, and the primary motivation was the promise of inexpensive electricity. In the 1950s and 1960s, the cost of uranium was very low in comparison with other fuels, and nuclear regulatory requirements were uncomplicated and straightforward. Although the cost of atomic energy has risen greatly in recent years, most utilities' preference for atomic energy may still be attributed to their evaluation of it as the most economically attractive source of power. One of the many utility-funded cost studies was recently released by the Electric Power Research Institute (EPRI), showing that nuclear power is less costly than coal-fired power generation, on the average, in every region of the United States.[32]

Behind their contention that nuclear power is economically desirable are two other more basic underlying attitudes that prevail among nuclear proponents and motivate their commitment to it. The industry is, by definition, comprised of technicians and scientists whose work consists of devising solutions to technical problems. Their own experience reinforces their belief in the potential solubility of those dilemmas. In other words, the members of the nuclear industry are scientific optimists convinced that any remaining safety questions associated with nuclear power can be solved technically, just as they feel all previous ones have been solved.

The second predominant and similar attitude is an avowal of the interrelationship of industrial growth and improved living standards. Those who perceive industrial expansion as the key to a better quality of life also insist that such expansion must involve increased energy usage. Without more energy, they claim, the have-nots can never achieve the same quality of life as the haves. Therefore, all available, economically viable energy sources are favored, and nuclear power, as one of the few such sources available on a large scale right now, is enthusiastically endorsed.

The nuclear industry's organizational framework is more structured than that of the antinuclear forces. The industry's most representative and active trade association is the Atomic Industrial Forum (AIF) founded in 1953. The AIF members include the thirty-seven or so utilities which own and operate nuclear power plants in the United States. Ten of these utilities produce over half of the nation's nuclear power and, in order of quantity of nuclear generating capacity, these are: Commonwealth Edison (Illinois), Tennessee Valley Authority (Southern states), Duke Power (North and South Carolina), Virginia Electric and Power (Virginia), Carolina Light and Power (North and South Carolina), Florida Power and Light (Florida), Northeast Utilities (Connecticut), Northern States Power (Minnesota), Baltimore Gas and Electric (Maryland), and Power Authority of the State of New York.[33] Commonwealth Edison is by far the largest with seven operating reactors.

In addition to the utilities, the other related parts of the nuclear industry are members of the AIF: the reactor manufacturers or vendors (General Electric Company, Westinghouse Electric Corporation, Babcock and Wilcox Company, and Combustion Engineering, Inc.); the architect-engineering firms which design and, in some cases, construct nuclear plants for the utilities (the major architect-engineering firms being Bechtel Corporation, Stone and Webster Engineering, Ebasco Services, Gibbs and Hill, Burns and Roe, Sargent and Lundy, Gilbert Associates, Pioneer Service and Engineers, and United Engineers and Constructors); the uranium mining companies (the largest being Gulf Oil, Kerr–McGee, Continental Oil, Exxon, Getty, Phelps Dodge–Western Nuclear, United Nuclear and Utah International); and other companies involved with some aspect of the nuclear fuel cycle. For example, the Board of Directors of the AIF includes representatives from the major private utilities, TVA, Westinghouse and General Electric, among others.

Along with a variety of technical functions, the AIF is a lobbying organization and has recently moved its headquarters to Washington in order to perform that role better. In addition, the AIF's output includes much information about nuclear power for public distribution by its member companies. It sometimes conducts seminars for company representatives to learn how to better promote atomic energy. The AIF also engages in public relations campaigns of its own and monitors antinuclear media output. For example, it tried unsuccessfully to persuade CBS to postpone an episode of the "Hawaii Five-O" series depicting terrorist construction of a crude atomic bomb until after the nuclear referendum vote in California in 1976.[34] The AIF publishes for the nuclear industry the *Nuclear Industry Magazine* and also a monthly newsletter, *INFO,* describing the political developments relevant to the future of atomic energy.

A second important trade association within the nuclear industry is the Edison Electric Institute (EEI), of which all the private, investor–owned utilities which produce 78 percent of the country's electricity are members. This association was formed in the 1930s to promote private ownership of utilities in the face of the increased number of federal and municipal power systems, and one of its current related functions is the encouragement of fossil (coal) and nuclear generation. Since all of the large utilities have committed themselves to nuclear plants, there is no question about their trade association's endorsement of atomic energy. Besides serving as a communications link for the utilities, the EEI funds electrical research, provides information and statistics on the industry and engages in national public relations efforts. It also encourages and guides the utilities in the conduct of their own marketing efforts, and it seeks to improve the industry's image through the distribution in schools of comic books and games. In recent years, EEI has done no governmental lobbying. However, in August, 1978, it merged with a separate lobbying group, the National Association of Electric Companies (NAEC); and lobbying is now one of the organization's responsibilities. Consequently, EEI has followed the lead of the AIF in moving its offices to Washington and trying to establish better governmental contact.

Besides the AIF and EEI, a third group with a vested interest in the development of nuclear power is the American Nuclear Society (ANS). The

ANS is a professional society with a membership of over 12,000, and it represents people employed in universities and government agencies as well as in corporations. Its monthly magazine *Nuclear News* discusses current technical, economic, and political issues and provides another source of information for the nuclear professionals. The ANS is now trying to encourage and facilitate individual political activism by distributing a newsletter about proposed Congressional legislation to the members of its new Nuclear Supporters Program. The ANS also has a lobbying arm called the American Nuclear Energy Council (ANEC), and it, too, publishes a newsletter. The ANEC acts as an information clearinghouse and aids the various industry lobbyists in Washington by developing common approaches, thereby making it the most effective political action organization.

Two additional sources of information about the nuclear industry are the periodical *Public Utilities Fortnightly,* which is distributed to utility executives, and the McGraw–Hill weekly newsletter called *Nucleonics Week*. The latter provides a gossipy, detailed account of the industry's current events and is probably the most widely read of the the industry publications.

The utilities themselves work for the promotion of nuclear power in a variety of ways. Company newsletters may discuss nuclear issues, provide rebuttals to critics of nuclear power and urge employees to contact government officials to express pronuclear views. Similarly, the electric companies sometimes do pronuclear public advertising in the media or in mailings to their customers when state regulatory agencies permit it. Utilities and other nuclear–related industries have also tried to carry the nuclear message to the public with participation by well–informed employees in company speakers' bureaus. Local organizations and schools can then request utility speakers for meetings to learn about nuclear power. Atomic plants themselves often contain Visitors' Information Centers which strive to allay concerns about nuclear energy. Finally, some utilities and most corporations involved in the nuclear industry have their own state and/or federal lobbyists, and funds for the campaign use of pronuclear legislators may come from the coffers of voluntary employee political action committees (PAC).

Certain industrial concerns, notably Westinghouse and General Electric, have had particularly active lobbyists and have done as much as the AIF to influence legislators. Westinghouse, for example, has carefully monitored energy legislation at the state and federal levels and has sent technical experts to testify at pertinent hearings and to inform key legislators. In an effort to generate pronuclear publicity, Westinghouse has distributed news releases, photos, and videotaped announcements to the media. In addition to its own speakers' bureaus and public information centers, Westinghouse has offered training and instructive printed matter and audiovisual aids for speakers from other companies in the nuclear industry.

Similar training seminars and pronuclear publishing have also been done by a consulting firm in Greenwich, Connecticut, called Reddy Communications, Inc., which sometimes works in coordination with Westinghouse.

Westinghouse has taken national opinion surveys on nuclear power quarterly since 1974 to try to determine the best target audiences and the key issues to address with pronuclear advertising. These public relations efforts were expanded during the 1976 state nuclear referenda votes. "State profiles" were compiled prior to each initiative which contained economic data, demographic statistics, legislative decisions and identification of the states' opinion leaders in politics, industry, labor, the media, ethnic and religious organizations, women's groups, and technical, academic, and professional associations. The statements of the leaders thus targeted were analyzed to determine their opinions so that their concerns could be addressed by the nuclear industry.[35] Westinghouse, along with the AIF, sought to coordinate and facilitate the nuclear industry's campaigns in each state prior to the initiatives.

Especially in the 1976 state initiative campaigns, the degree of cohesion of the nuclear industry was very great. In fact, with the exception of the well-publicized engineers who defected from General Electric during the California campaign, the concurrence regarding atomic energy has been nearly unanimous. This has been true in spite of frequent corporate disputes of a financial nature. One such dispute began in October, 1976, when Westinghouse Electric Corporation filed antitrust suits against twenty-nine uranium producers, charging them with having formed a cartel to raise fuel prices artificially. At the same time, twenty-seven utilities that had contracts to buy uranium from Westinghouse prior to the cartel's price hike then took Westinghouse to court when that company backed out of its uranium supply commitments.[36] Similarly, there are frequent price disputes between the architect-engineers and other firms which design, supply, or construct power plants and the client utilities that have hired them. For example, in August, 1974, Consumers Power Company filed suit against five firms involved with the Palisades nuclear plant (Combustion Engineering, Bechtel Corporation, Bechtel Company, Ingersoll-Rand Company and Wolverine Tube Company), later settling the suit out-of-court for cash and services amounting to between $40 million and $60 million in damages.[37] However, such corporate disputes are usually impersonal in nature and do not ordinarily engender rancorous interpersonal relationships. Nor do they seem to affect the industry's ability to work as a unit for public relations and lobbying purposes.

The most obvious resource at the disposal of the nuclear industry would seem to be money. However, the economic stability of the corporate components that comprise the nuclear industry is not as great as one would expect. Because of the significant decline in the number of atomic plants ordered and built in the 1970s, there has been a corresponding decline in the economic health of the nuclear industry.

From the mid-1960s through the early 1970s, when the annual electric growth rate averaged 7 percent, the utilities placed orders for large numbers of nuclear plants. In 1973, for instance, forty-one nuclear plants were planned.[38] However, the inflationary spiral of the late 1960s and early 1970s drove up the cost of the plants that were ordered, as did the increasing regulatory requirements. Then came the recession of 1974 and, with it, the temporary negative electric growth rate that hurt utility revenues and made them unable to finance construction projects, especially at the high interest rates that followed the recession. The utilities began canceling or postponing many of their previous power plant orders, especially atomic plants. The cost of atomic plants had especially increased for a variety of reasons: nuclear plants require the largest capital expenditures of any power plants; there had been a rise in the price of uranium;[39] and the nuclear plants were more frequently beset by regulatory and court-ordered delays in their construction and operation. Utilities found it particularly difficult to afford the atomic plants they had ordered before the recession.

The result of these factors was a significant reduction in the number of atomic plants ordered. In 1974, the utilities canceled nine nuclear units and postponed ninety-one others. In 1975, there were twelve cancellations and eighty-six deferrals. In 1976 and the first half of 1977, eight reactor orders were canceled and 106 units deferred.[40] Of the sixty-five plants ordered in 1976, only three were nuclear.[41] There were no authentic nuclear plant orders in 1977,[42] and 1978 ended with just two new reactors ordered. Furthermore, the big backlog of work left over from 1973 to 1974 has almost been completed, and nuclear-related firms have long since begun laying off technical personnel and searching for nonnuclear work. One of the five reactor manufacturers in the country, General Atomic, a subsidiary of Gulf Oil Corporation and the Royal Dutch/Shell group, actually withdrew from the market in 1975; and, in May of 1977, General Electric, one of the two largest manufacturers, threatened to do the same thing.[43] Thus, the economic future of the nuclear industry as a whole has become tenuous.

The nuclear industry's investment in atomic power and the nuclear fuel cycle was estimated in 1975 to be over $100 billion.[44] It is now far more than than, with nearly $6 billion spent in 1978 alone on nuclear plant construction.[45] When an industrial commitment takes on such large proportions, it is self-perpetuating and cumulative in nature. By advocating nuclear power, the industry strives to protect its investment. There is no question about the fact that the companies in the nuclear industry would suffer severe financial difficulty from the abandonment of atomic energy.

It is important to realize, however, that none of the larger component parts of the nuclear industry are wholly dependent upon atomic energy. In

1978, for example, with the exception of only three small utilities, the power companies in the United States had the major portion of their operating capacity for electric generation in nonnuclear plants;[46] the architect engineering firms also designed fossil-fired plants; reactor manufacturers ("vendors") produced equipment for non-nuclear plants; and the majority of the large uranium mining firms were primarily oil companies. Consequently, in the battle over the future of nuclear power, these companies are probably not fighting for their ultimate survival. Perhaps as a result, the extent of their commitment of resources to the pro-nuclear cause has usually been fairly limited.

When the nuclear industry has been directly and obviously threatened, as was the case in the 1976 state referendum campaigns to restrict the development of atomic energy, the industry has been willing to commit funds in self-defense. During the state initiative efforts in 1976, the industry spent $11.8 million on opposition to antinuclear referenda, as compared with $1.9 million from the environmental groups.[47] However, state legislatures have sometimes set a ceiling on the amount that corporations could contribute to initiative campaigns, as they did in California. Even without state referendum proposals, some pronuclear advertising is being done, especially by Westinghouse, General Electric, Gulf, and Exxon. However, most of the utilities have allocated very little funding to public relations efforts on behalf of nuclear power. They are often deterred from certain forms of advertising by state public utility commissions' prohibitions and by the utilities' reluctance to claim the advertising as a business expense. Furthermore, in the absence of an obvious threat, such as the state initiatives presented, they have difficulty justifying economically the expenditure of much time and money on public relations.

A handicap from which the industry suffers is its lack of an active minority of a few obvious, long-term leaders who have primary influence over policy decisions, act as spokespersons for the industry, and are known media figures. The managerial head of the AIF is a physicist named Carl Walske who, with his staff, accepts the policy suggestions from the corporate representatives who constitute the board of directors. The EEI also has a professional staff, but its chairmanship is elective and rotates among the heads of its member utilities. Consequently, there are a large number of nuclear industry leaders, some more influential than others, but none who have become highly visible, dominant figures in the various trade associations. This is probably due to the fact that, as mentioned previously, none of the companies that comprise the nuclear industry (except for very small ones) are totally involved in it, and the nuclear issue is only one of several concerns that have salience for those corporate leaders. Consequently, none of them are real political activists in regard to the promotion of the development of atomic energy.

Because it lacks obvious leadership, the nuclear interest group has relied upon scientists, academicians or government agency heads to be its surrogate spokespersons, such as Edward Teller (who helped invent the hydrogen bomb), Norman Rasmussen (the professor who chairs the Nuclear Engineering Department at the Massachusetts Institute of Technology and directed the Commission's Reactor Safety Study released in October, 1975), or Dixy Lee Ray (former Atomic Energy Commission chairperson and now Governor of the State of Washington). The problem with such spokespersons, of course, is that they do not always concur with all the industry's positions and, in fact, usually go to great lengths to demonstrate their financial and intellectual dissociation from the nuclear industry, while advocating the development of atomic energy.

Perhaps because of the absence of activist, visible leadership in the nuclear industry, the interest group has not taken full advantage of the various political strategies available to influence nuclear power policymaking. The industry has most often engaged in the traditional forms of lobbying and has, in the past, largely refrained from utilizing other more innovative tactics. For instance, the enormous number of employees involved in the nuclear-related firms, as well as the stockholders of those companies and even the companies' pensioners, have rarely been recruited for political action: letter-writing to officials, campaign work, political donations, and other grassroots lobbying efforts. This manpower source was well organized and effectively mobilized during the 1976 state referenda campaigns. However, the alliance of pronuclear forces that was forged in California, for example, has since become disorganized.[48] Without the direct threat of antinuclear state initiatives, the industry's manpower has not been politicized on a continuing basis. Company newsletters and political action groups, as well as trade association groups of the kinds mentioned previously, are just now slowly starting to tap this source of industry strength on a regular basis, without the impetus of state initiatives.

Another organizational resource which the nuclear industry has not fully utilized is its potential formation of coalitions with a variety of other interest groups. Organized labor, with the notable exception of the United Auto Workers, is usually quite supportive of the industry. At the EEI convention in June, 1977, Robert Georgine, a representative of the AFL-CIO, expressed his support for economic growth fueled by nuclear power. He estimated that the cost of prohibiting further development of atomic energy would be the loss of 1½ million jobs.[49] In February, 1977, the AFL-CIO Executive Council issued an energy statement urging that "Every effort must be made to accelerate the development of coal and nuclear power . . . [and] the record of the nuclear industry [in safety] is among the best in all industry."[50] Labor has sometimes come to the political aid of the industry, as in California, where the construction trade unions were part of the pronuclear forces. At Seabrook, New Hampshire also, it was the local of the Plumbers and Pipefitters Union in Manchester, New Hampshire, along with many union members' wives in the New Hampshire Voice of Energy organization, that was largely responsible for recruiting 3,000 people to attend the pronuclear rally on June 26, 1977.[51] However, at the national level, the unions have not exercised their considerable political influence on the pronuclear side. Furthermore, there was some visible defection of union support to the antinuclear point of view after the Three Mile Island accident.

A public alliance of some blacks with the nuclear industry is in the developmental stage. Bayard Rustin, President of the A. Philip Randolph Institute, has opposed a no-growth policy on the grounds that economic growth is the only means of creating greater equality in American society.[52] This perspective was later espoused by the NAACP Energy Conference in November, 1977, which was chaired by Dr. Margaret Bush Wilson. The Carter Energy Plan of 1977 was criticized by the NAACP for its limits-to-growth philosophy and for ''a myriad of government constraints on. . . nuclear power . . . . ''[53] The Conference report endorsed the use of atomic energy as a source of electricity[54] and, thereby, reflected a new policy stand that is not universally shared by blacks, especially by the National Urban League.

Another resource that has been available to the nuclear industry has been legal expertise. Each component company in the industry has its own legal staff, and the funds for litigation are available. When the utilities find themselves involved in litigation regarding nuclear plants, they usually supplement their own legal talent by hiring one of the traditional law firms to represent them in court. Le Boeuf, Lamb, Leiby, and MacRae is one of several firms that is especially active in legal work for the nuclear industry.

Very recently there have developed public interest law groups that support the development of nuclear power. One of these, the Pacific Legal Foundation, is based in Sacramento, California, with an auxiliary office in Washington, D.C. A similar and larger organization is the National Legal Center for the Public Interest (NLCPI) which began in 1975. Although it sponsors no litigation itself, the NLCPI acts as a catalyst and clearinghouse for the litigation of its eight affiliated regional groups. Thus far, these pronuclear public interest law firms have usually contributed friend-of-the-court briefs to existing litigation, rather than filing suits themselves. Like their counterpart public interest law firms that support environmental causes, the Pacific Legal Foundation and the NLCPI and its affiliates are nonprofit organizations. Their support comes from foundations, individuals, and corporations. Thus, the organizational frameworks and resources for litigation are just as available for the use of the nuclear industry as they are for the antinuclear groups.

Summary and Conclusions

A comparison of the interest groups in the nuclear power controversy shows that the nuclear industry has not significantly benefited from an organization that is more structured than that of the antinuclear environmentalists. The antinuclear groups are just as cohesive as the industry, and both sets of groups have consistent ideological perspectives and good communications networks.

In regard to financial resources, neither interest group spends large amounts of money on political action. In the case of the nuclear industry, economic setbacks in the 1970s have undermined its financial stability. In addition, none of the large companies that comprise the nuclear industry depend totally upon its further development for their own survival, which is another reason why their commitment of resources for pronuclear political action has usually been relatively small. Furthermore, state public utility commissions frequently restrict utilities' political expenditures. As for the antinuclear groups, they experience the same financial constraints as other public interest groups. However, both the industry and the environmentalists have the organizations and resources necessary for the use of litigation.

The major disparity between the resources of the two sets of interest groups involves their respective leadership. The antinuclear groups benefit from visible, activist leaders who have a strong personal commitment to their cause. Because of the leaders' organizational ability and political acumen, they have done better than the nuclear industry in mobilizing support from members and coalition groups. The leadership of the nuclear industry, on the other hand, is diffuse and fragmented because its corporate heads have usually not regarded the commitment to the further development of atomic power as their companies' top priority. Probably as a result, there are few well-known spokespersons or visible political activists for whom the nuclear power issue has primary salience. Not surprisingly, the industry's supporters are infrequently mobilized, and its potential coalition support is underutilized.

Nonetheless, the outcome of a policymaking controversy depends not only on the nature of the interest groups but also on the characteristics of the governmental institutions they wish to influence and the strategies used to gain support. It is evident that both sets of interest groups in the nuclear controversy utilize many political strategies, but the antinuclear groups use a wider variety of traditional and nontraditional tactics to influence policy decisions. This disparity in tactics will be examined through a description of the interest groups' involvement of the judiciary in nuclear power policymaking.

3 The Role of the Nuclear Regulatory Commission

One hundred and fifty years ago, Alexis de Tocqueville remarked, "Scarcely any political question arises in the United States that is not resolved sooner or later into a judicial question."[1] In the last two decades, the development of nuclear power has been effectively transformed from a technical and economic question into a political one; and, as such, interest groups have brought it before the courts repeatedly.

Since the Commission (formerly the Atomic Energy Commission and now the Nuclear Regulatory Commission) is the agency that establishes the nuclear plant regulatory standards and also issues the plant licenses, the suits are most often, but not always, filed against the Commission. However, judicial review may not occur until the Commission has completed its rulings, and environmental groups must have intervened in the Commission's licensing or rulemaking hearings in order to be able to appeal the Commission's decisions to the courts. Thus, the Commission is a quasi-judicial body, and its decision making represents the initial phase in the judicial policymaking process regarding atomic plants.

The use of legal advocacy as an interest group strategy is dependent upon more variables than just the groups' organizational frameworks and resources for litigation. In matters that involve regulatory agency rulings, such as the development of nuclear power plants, the decision to use legal advocacy also depends upon the interest groups' attitudes toward the Commission and its decision making. This chapter will describe those attitudes and the interrelationships between the interest groups and the Commission as factors which encourage or deter the groups from appeals of administrative rulings to the courts.

The Commission's Statutory Role

After the Atomic Energy Commission (AEC) was abolished by the Energy Reorganization Act of 1974, the Nuclear Regulatory Commission (NRC) was organized to take responsibility for regulation of nuclear power plants. The Commission is composed of five civilian commissioners, one of whom is the chairman, and all are appointed by the President, subject to Senate confirmation. These commissioners have a large supporting staff working in the three major departments of the Commission: the Office of Nuclear

Reactor Regulation which issues rules and licenses for nuclear plants, the Office of Nuclear Regulatory Research which engages in technical research, and the Office of Nuclear Material Safety and Safeguards which handles fuel regulation.

The procedures for the regulation and licensing of atomic plants were outlined in the Atomic Energy Act amendments of 1954. They require that, as with other regulatory agencies, the Commission use two different policy-making processes: *rulemaking* and *adjudication*. Rulemaking refers to generic decision making by the Commission in regard to general standards for all nuclear plants. Rulemaking procedures are usually legislative in nature in that testimony may be presented by interested parties other than the hearing board, but the parties are not allowed to cross-examine or respond to each other's testimony. The formal rulemaking process allows oral comments, while informal rulemaking specifies that comments be written. In recent years, however, the strictly legislative aspects of rulemaking have been diluted in some hybrid or quasi-judicial hearings in which cross-examination has been allowed.

Adjudication is the other procedure used by regulatory agencies for their decision making, and the Commission relies on the adjudication process for its licensing of nuclear plants. Licensing by adjudication is done on a case-by-case basis for each individual plant, and the procedure resembles that of a judicial trial. Public testimony and cross-examination are part of the adjudication process, as will be explained.

Before describing the statutory procedure with which individual nuclear plants are licensed by the Commission, it should be noted that not only the Commission but also a variety of other federal, state, and local agencies also issue licenses for various facets of nuclear plants. In fact, each plant may be required to apply for as many as sixty different licenses. However, only the two licenses which the Commission must issue for each plant are under examination here; and the acquisition of these is the major hurdle which each atomic plant must overcome.

The Commission's plant licensing involves a two-step process: first, a construction permit must be issued before a plant is built; next, an operating license is issued before the reactor begins generating electricity. The Atomic Energy Act of 1954 entitled citizens to intervene individually or collectively before the Commission prior to the issuance of a construction permit, but the public hearings were originally optional. Revisions of the Act in 1957 made these public hearings an automatic part of the licensing process. In 1962, a further statutory change authorized public hearings before the issuance of the operating license, as well. The Commission must give public notice of intent to issue an operating license and must conduct public hearings if the public petitions for them. Consequently, there are now two points in the licensing process for intervention, with the public hearings prior to nuclear plant construction being mandatory; and the second set of hearings prior to plant operation occurring only at the petition of intervenors.

The utility that intends to build a nuclear power plant must provide literally volumes of information regarding the proposed plant for the Commission to review. First, the utility submits a lengthy application for a construction permit. The Commission staff appraises the technical and financial qualifications of the utility, as well as the specific design of the reactor, its quality control system, the adequacy of plant safety and auxiliary systems, and the results of various accident analyses based on possible and hypothetical plant malfunctions. The application is also reviewed "from the point of view of location, meteorology, geology, hydrology, seismicity . . . and the environmental impact."[2] The staff then identifies specific problems, requests additional information, and, finally, holds extended informal meetings with the applicant to negotiate terms by which the staff can support the application. The utility is usually directed to make various alterations in its nuclear plant design, and it must satisfy the Commission staff's demands before the plant application is accepted. Thus, the Commission and the utility have reached an agreement on the various aspects of the plant's construction before the public hearings process occurs.

At the conclusion of the staff review, the Advisory Committee on Reactor Safeguards (ACRS) makes an independent technical review of the permit to identify its novel aspects. The ACRS is a committee created by Congressional statute to provide an opinion independent of the Commission's opinion and, thereby, act as a check on the Commission staff. The ACRS is composed of a maximum of fifteen scientifically-trained experts who are appointed on a part-time basis by the Commission. The ACRS issues a public report concerning its evaluation of the safety of each proposed nuclear plant.

The ACRS report and the Commission staff evaluation are both submitted to the Atomic Safety and Licensing Board (ASLB). The three-person ASLB is composed of two technical experts (one in nuclear and one in environmental sciences) and a presiding officer with administrative experience, usually an attorney, chosen from a panel selected by the Commission. If outside individuals or groups have contested the construction permit, the ASLB must make an independent evaluation of the application, as well as of the Commission staff and ACRS reports. The ASLB then conducts public hearings at which intervenors present their criticisms of the construction permit application. Following the hearings, a permit may be authorized by the ASLB. Although the ASLB permit goes into effect immediately, intervenors may appeal the ASLB decision to the Atomic Safety and Licensing Appeal Board (ASLAB) which is also composed of three members with the same types of expertise as the ASLB panel. Their decision on the plant permit is supposed to be the final one in the administrative review process. However, the five Commissioners may, on their own initiative, reassess a license application and make a final ruling themselves, thereby superseding the ASLB decision.

After the start of the plant's construction, the Commission staff continues to monitor the nuclear plant on an on-going basis. Well before the time that the plant is ready to begin generating electricity, the utility submits an application for an operating license which, again, is reviewed by the Commission staff and the ACRS. Again, problem areas are resolved informally between the utility and the regulators. The utility must accede to Commission requests for changes in the plant if it is to receive the staff's approval of the operating license. Having satisfied the Commission staff and the ACRS, the utility has their agreement regarding its application prior to the optional public hearings process. At this stage, when public hearings are requested, as now they always are, the ASLB again conducts them and makes the determination regarding the issuance of an operating license. Again, the ASLB ruling can be appealed to the ASLAB which then makes the final licensing decision unless the Commissioners object to it.

The public hearings for a plant's construction permit or operating license involve adjudication, an adversary proceeding set up much like a trial court. The license applicant acts as the defendant and bears the "burden of proof"[3] in testimony that the plant will not harm public health or safety. The public interest group(s) or representative(s) act as prosecutors in their role as full intervenors. They may submit their own testimony and witnesses, or they may cross-examine and question the utility representative. It is the ASLB that serves as the trial judge, conducting the proceedings and ruling on the license application.

Although a complete examination of the administrative process will not be undertaken here, it should be noted that it is largely dominated by the legal staffs of the utility and the public interest groups opposing the proposed plant. As one observer has noted, "The ASLB hearings are designed by lawyers evidently for the convenience of lawyers."[4] The hearings are intended to resolve technical and scientific questions, but the adversary nature of the proceedings has necessitated that lawyers play a pivotal role: presenting the cases, determining the issues, and cross-examining the witnesses. The lawyers frequently have technical advisors at the hearings to assist them in their questioning. However, because the lawyers generally lack full understanding of the technical issues under consideration, they tend to concentrate on procedural matters. Consequently, the technical matters are often lost amidst the "legal gymnastics" and "procedural wrangling."[5]

The primacy of the lawyers' role in the hearings process is noted here in order to provide a backdrop to the importance of the same lawyers in their continuing role of interest group representation within the courts. After the Commission has issued either a construction permit or an operating license for a nuclear plant, the intervenors can and often do appeal the Commission's decision to the judiciary. Thus, court cases become merely an extension of the administrative process. Although the Commission hearings are expected to resolve technical questions and the judiciary is likely to determine statutory compliance and review administrative procedures, actually the Commission is frequently concerned with procedural problems and the courts often find themselves involved in substantive issues. Consequently, the demarcation line between agency hearings and court cases is obscure because the same participants and issues appear in each setting. The same procedures which the lawyers contested in the administrative licensing hearings are the ones that become the legal questions which they appeal to the courts.

Commission licenses and generic regulations regarding nuclear power plants may be appealed to the courts as a result of Section 189(b) of the Atomic Energy Act of 1954. It specifies that Commission decisions should be reviewed according to the manner prescribed in the Administrative Procedure Act of 1946.[6] The Administrative Procedure Act authorizes the courts to compel the Commission and other agencies to act, and it also allows the courts to set aside agency decisions. Through the Administrative Procedure Act, Congress gave the court responsibility for reviewing regulatory decisions that fall into one of three categories: first, decisions that are "not in accordance with law"; secondly, decisions that seem "arbitrary, capricious, [or] an abuse of discretion"; and thirdly, decisions "unsupported by substantial evidence." Thus, the first criterion for judicial review is that of agency violation of a statute or of legislative intent, and the second one involves unreasonable actions taken by an agency. The third criterion involves procedural failings on the part of the agency, such as failure to obtain sufficient evidence or hold the proper hearings before reaching a conclusion.[7] Because of the Administrative Procedure Act, the courts have frequently ruled that "an agency or commission must articulate with clarity and precision its findings and the reasons for its decision."[8] The Commission must carefully explain the rationale behind its regulations and licensing.

The Act provides, however, that before bringing a case to court, the litigant must have exhausted all possible administrative remedies. After the regulatory agency procedures are exhausted, according to Section 10(a) of the Act, " . . . a person suffering legal wrong because of agency action within the meaning of a relevant statute is entitled to judicial review thereof." Consequently, the courts try to avoid judicial action that might be premature. In at least two cases, the courts have refused to hear contentions against the Commission's licensing procedures on the grounds that the administrative process was not exhausted when the charges were filed.[9]

Were it not for the mandate of the Administrative Procedure Act and the governmental administrative apparatus to which it applies, there would be little or no basis for litigation against nuclear power plants. The nuclear industry is, like most businesses, an amorphous group of interrelated components. Therefore, decisions regarding investment, policy, and operations are made in a manner that is "general, diffuse, and legally insulated [and] while business decisions viewed collectively have vast differential effects on social groups, these are the result of decisions made discretely, seriatim, for profit, by hundreds of individuals and companies."[10] The Commission has provided the tangible structure through which the antinuclear groups can directly confront the industry first in administrative hearings and, later, in court. It is the Commission's statutory charter to safeguard public health and safety that makes it provide a forum for public criticism of industry decisions. When the environmental groups bring suit against the industry, it is because the Commission has crystallized the industry into a tangible "party" by making it subject to regulation. Thus, the Commission's role makes it the vehicle through which the contending interest groups in the atomic energy controversy initially confront each other. The groups' relations with the Commission largely determine whether the groups decide to subject the nuclear power issues to litigation.

Interest Group Relations with the Commission

Using the administrative framework and the statutory basis for litigation, it is incumbent upon the interest groups involved in the nuclear power controversy to initiate lawsuits if they want to include the judiciary in the nuclear power policymaking process. Legal advocacy has always been a strategy used by interest groups, but its importance has grown in recent years. The activism of the Warren Court in the 1950s and 1960s encouraged groups to seek legal remedies for social problems. The more activist the judiciary, the more likely it is that groups will become involved in litigation. As Truman points out, "A judiciary with power will inevitably be an object of the struggle for control."[11] However, in spite of the allure of judicial endorsement, the antinuclear environmental groups in the nuclear power controversy have been more inclined to use legal advocacy as a significant interest-group strategy than has the nuclear industry.

The Commission plays a pivotal role in determining the attitudes of the interest groups toward the use of legal advocacy. Since the judicial review of Commission decisions is dependent upon the Commission's completion of its decision-making process, the relationship of the interest groups to the Commission in the course of that process is an important determinant of their inclination to appeal the decision.

The antinuclear groups have traditionally distrusted the Commission and considered its rulings to be biased toward the nuclear industry. Therefore, it is not surprising that those groups have taken advantage of the statutory provision for judicial review of Commission decisions. In so doing, the antinuclear groups are like other public interest groups, according to David Vogel who asserts that the public interest movement is especially predisposed toward appealing to the judiciary.[12]

Part of the attraction of litigation for public interest groups is their perception of the court as an impartial adjudicator. Judges are esteemed and considered to be free from economic and political pressures. As Joseph Sax expressed it, " . . . the court preeminently is a forum where the individual citizen or community group can obtain a hearing on equal terms with the highly organized and experienced interests that have learned so skillfully to manipulate legislative and administrative interests."[13] Furthermore, judges lack technical expertise and are "generalists" by training. Public interest groups expect, therefore, that they stand a better chance when they appeal to the judges' concern for intangible societal values than when they bring their case before the Commission.

When the AEC was in existence, the antinuclear groups considered the regulatory agency to be subject to the "capture" theory: that is, the agency seemed to the environmentalists to be a captive of its clientele, the nuclear industry. The Commission's critics charged that it acted according to its mandate to promote the development of atomic energy at the expense of its other responsibility: the protection of public health and safety. The environmentalists frequently took their concerns to Congress, but at least initially, to no avail.

Consequently, the courts provided another forum in which to criticize nuclear power development; and judicial decisions could potentially act as a catalyst for Congressional legislation more favorable to environmental concerns. As Jeffrey Berry has commented, it is not unusual for public interest groups to view litigation primarily as a means of influencing other governmental institutions.[14] In regard to nuclear power litigation, the environmental groups used legal advocacy to influence both the AEC and Congress.

In spite of the fact that the AEC has been disbanded and the NRC has assumed its regulatory functions, the antinuclear groups still charge that the NRC continues to be as much of a "promoting agency" as the AEC.[15] By setting standards for nuclear power and issuing licenses for the plants, the agency is implicitly sanctioning the development of nuclear power when the antinuclear groups believe its development should be halted altogether. The environmentalists contend further that the Commission remains a captive of the nuclear industry since 65 percent of its senior personnel came to work there from "private enterprises holding licenses, permits or contracts from the NRC."[16] Therefore, in the opinion of the nuclear opponents, "The NRC . . . accepts as its own guidelines, standards which are written by industry committees."[17] In view of their conviction that the Commission is biased in favor of nuclear power, it is not surprising that environmental groups have often resorted to legal advocacy to appeal the Commission rulings.

The nuclear industry has not followed the environmental groups' propensity to use legal advocacy because its relationship with the Commission has been very different. When the AEC was in existence, it shared the nuclear industry's aspirations for the rapid expansion of atomic power and, in fact, had been largely responsible for promoting those aspirations and encouraging the industry's development. The utilities could count on the Commission to facilitate their development of nuclear plants through expeditious licensing and rulemaking procedures and a stable regulatory climate. Therefore, utility lawyers had no reason to be aggressive and initiate litigation: "Before 1970 the average utility's lawyer was a sluggish guy who pushed a tall stack of papers through the regulatory agencies. For him, the process was a matter of time, not substance."[18]

The nuclear industry's relationship to the NRC is very different, however. The industry believes that the Commission no longer plays a supportive role. Two of the new commissioners have the backing of the environmental groups, and one of them is particularly vocal in his criticism of the current nuclear plant licensing process. Because of the new appointees and Congressional pressures on the Commission, there is a notable lack of cohesiveness within the Commission's governing body and no clear consensus regarding proper regulatory procedures. The ambivalence of the commissioners and staff is reflected in the Commission's lengthy and indecisive regulatory proceedings.

The nuclear industry complains that the Commission's requirements for atomic plants change frequently, and the new standards are often accompanied by orders for their retroactive application to existing plants and designs. In addition, the Commission has expanded its procedural format for licensing nuclear plants, and the total time allotment for building and licensing a nuclear plant now ranges from twelve to fourteen years. The combination of changing standards and lengthy proceedings has greatly added to the cost for utilities in developing nuclear plants, leading the industry to charge that the Commission's requirements are largely responsible for the decline in utility orders for the plants.[19]

Nonetheless, the nuclear industry has been reluctant to use legal advocacy to initiate judicial review of the Commission's procedures and rulings. The industry has had similar reluctance to file suits against other federal, state or local agencies such as the public utility commissions, for example, that have handed down unfavorable rulings. The explanation for the industry's legal reticence probably lies in its concern about reprisals: the industry has not deliberately antagonized the bodies that are responsible for its regulation since they may retaliate by withholding needed licenses, rate increases, and site approvals. The utilities are dependent upon the governmental regulatory bodies for permission to generate and sell power, so they try not to undermine whatever goodwill the members of those bodies may feel toward them. Therefore, in spite of the nuclear industry's dissatisfaction with the Commission, it is not inclined toward the use of legal advocacy.

Summary and Conclusions

It is evident that the nature of the nuclear power plant licensing process facilitates intervention by antinuclear environmental groups. According to the Atomic Energy Act, the Commission's licensing procedures provide two separate points at which environmental groups may contest a plant's development: first, at the construction permit hearings and, later, at the operating license hearings. At each of these points, the antinuclear groups may appeal the Atomic Safety and Licensing Board's ruling to the Atomic Safety and Licensing Appeal Board upon the conclusion of the hearings process. Then, if they desire, the Commissioners themselves may review the Appeal Board's ruling. Finally, under the provisions of the Administrative Procedure Act, the Commission's decision may be sent to the courts for judicial review.

Thus, on this issue involving high-risk technology, antinuclear public interest groups have the advantage of ample statutory opportunity to challenge and delay bureaucratic decision making. Furthermore, because they believe that the Atomic Energy Commission and its successor, the Nuclear Regulatory Commission, have been captives of the nuclear industry, they charge that the Commission has inadequately performed its regulatory functions. Consequently, the environmental groups have an adversary relationship with the Commission and are inclined to use legal advocacy and appeal Commission rulings to the courts.

The nuclear industry, on the other hand, previously felt that the Atomic Energy Commission was serving its best interests. However, Nuclear Regulatory Commission decision making has been less supportive of nuclear power development, as evidenced by the period of twelve to fourteen years now required for the licensing process. The nuclear industry is now as critical of the performance of the Commission as the antinuclear groups. Nevertheless, the clientele industry, as the license applicant, tends to remain deferential to the Commission in the hope of engendering no antagonism which might further delay the licensing process. It is not surprising, therefore, that the nuclear industry, consisting mostly of utilities, has avoided the initiation of litigation against the Commission and other regulatory bodies while the environmentalists have frequently chosen legal advocacy as an interest group strategy. The results of this one-sided use of legal advocacy remain to be examined.

4

The Role of the Judiciary in Nuclear Power Cases

As a prelude to the case study of the Midland nuclear plant litigation, this chapter will provide an overview of other major nuclear power cases that have arisen since the development of commercial atomic energy plants. These major judicial opinions provide the precedents that are cited in the Midland case and other current nuclear plant rulings. They represent the collective policy output from two decades of judicial policymaking.

In all the years of litigation concerning the development of atomic energy plants, the nuclear industry has initiated only one of the major nuclear power suits. Thus, the antinuclear environmental groups have had almost exclusive use of the tactic of legal advocacy, and the advantages of this interest group strategy will be described. In addition, the policy impact from the judicial process will be given an initial assessment in terms of its effect on the interest group litigants.

Major Judicial Rulings

Having chosen legal advocacy as a major antinuclear strategy, the environmental groups' most significant accomplishment has been the increase in judicial involvement in environmental matters through the liberalization of the doctrine of *standing*. The impact of liberalized standing requirements is evidenced by the fact that while "environment" was not even one of the formal legal categories in *U.S. Law Week* reports until 1969–1970, it is now one of the most frequent items on the judicial docket.[1] Without standing, environmental groups could not file suits contesting nuclear power plant licenses and standards. Therefore, opponents of nuclear power, along with other public interest groups, have taken full advantage of the courts' willingness to give them standing and accept the litigation they initiate.

The standing doctrine is one of the judiciary's mechanisms for limiting the types and numbers of cases that come before it. Standing means access to court action or "the rules governing who may bring suit, with respect to which official actions."[2] Article III of the United States Constitution provides that courts limit themselves to consideration of actual cases or controversies, meaning that the party bringing suit must have suffered an actual wrong or legal injury. The ambiguity of the Constitution has left it to the discretion of the courts to define what constitutes a case or controversy and to determine who has been wronged. Since both judicial appraisals are subjective, the interpretation of the Constitutional limits on judicial decision making has varied through the years according to the political conditions and predilections of the era. The judiciary has recently liberalized its doctrine of standing to allow more cases to be subject to judicial review.

In the process of liberalizing standing, the judiciary has expanded its definition of injury. In previous years, primarily physical injuries to an individual or economic injuries to private property were considered to be sufficient grounds for bringing suit against government agencies. Since 1965, however, the definition of injury has been enlarged to include injury to intangible values, such as concern for aesthetics or the environment. In *Scenic Hudson Preservation Conference* v. *FPC,*[3] the court of appeals ruled that a conservation group had standing to appeal a Federal Power Commission ruling to the court as a result of its aesthetic values.[4] A public interest group was again given standing and recognition of the importance of its noneconomic values by another court of appeals in 1966 in the case of *Office of Communications of the United Church of Christ* v. *FCC.*[5] Then, in 1970, the test of injury as a condition for standing was satisfied by a coalition of environmental organizations in *Environmental Defense Fund* v. *Hardin* in which the court of appeals held that "demonstrated interest in protecting the environment from pesticide pollution was sufficient to satisfy the injury–in–fact test."[6]

In 1972, however, the Supreme Court ruled that organizational standing was dependent upon injuries incurred by the organization's membership.[7] In *Sierra Club* v. *Morton,*[8] the Court's opinion indicated that an organization must prove its genuine interest in the matter under litigation and show that its own members were adversely affected. A year after the *Sierra Club* v. *Morton* ruling, the Supreme Court said in *U.S.* v. *Students Challenging Regulatory Agency Procedures [SCRAP]*[9] that the group's standing was dependent upon its membership's recreational use of the environment. Now standing is so freely granted to groups representing environmental interests that the concept of standing has practically lost its legal significance. Many legalists approve of the easing of standing requirements[10] and feel that the effort and financial commitment entailed in bringing suit are in and of themselves sufficient to demonstrate a special interest in the matter under judicial review.[11]

The courts' grant of standing to other environmental and public interest groups has, likewise, made it possible for antinuclear groups to secure adjudication of their concerns without difficulty. The judiciary usually grants standing in nuclear power cases to groups that have intervened in the Commission's regulatory process. It is the prerogative of the Commission to determine which persons or groups are potentially affected by the nuclear plant and to grant them the right to intervene in the hearings. The Commission usually puts few requirements on intervenors except that they "identify the specific aspect or aspects of the subject matter of the proceeding as to which intervention is sought and particularize the basis for the contentions," a requirement that the court upheld in *BPI* v. *AEC*.[12] Regulatory intervention then leads easily to the grant of standing before the courts.

The grant of standing has not conferred on antinuclear groups court-ordered compensation for legal expenses. Since the local groups which ordinarily protest individual nuclear plants are typically small in membership and short of funds, they have frequently sought court-ordered financial compensation. There is precedent for such public interest group financing through the legal concept of private attorneys-general or "individuals regarded as vindicating the public interest by bringing suit against government officials who had acted in an extra-statutory manner." However, in cases such as *Citizens for a Safe Environment* v. *AEC*,[13] the courts have refused to extend the "private attorneys-general" concept to antinuclear groups. This judicial policy was affirmed in *Alyeska Pipeline Service Co.* v. *Wilderness Society*,[14] a nonnuclear case. The Supreme Court ruled that financial compensation would be awarded only when suits concern the enforcement of statutes that specifically provide for such compensation.

In order to halt the construction and/or operation of individual plants and of nuclear power in general, public interest groups have hung their antinuclear court suits on a wide variety of legalistic pegs. Their lawsuits have challenged the Commission's procedural methodology, its jurisdictional scope, and its statutory compliance.

Safety standards have frequently been the issue under contention in environmental lawsuits. The first antinuclear litigation was initiated in 1956 in the case of *Power Reactor Development Co.* v. *International Union of Electric, Radio and Machine Workers*.[15] The labor union contested the construction permit issued for an experimental fast breeder reactor near Detroit, the Fermi plant. Under adjudication was the Commission's ruling that issuance of a construction permit could proceed without consideration of some safety issues and that these issues could be postponed until the operating licence hearings. The Court of Appeals of the District of Columbia set aside the Commission's ruling and remanded it.[16] However, on appeal, the Supreme Court upheld the Commission procedure, saying, "We see no reason why we should not accord to the Commission's interpretation of its own regulation and governing statute that respect which is customarily given to a practical administrative construction of a disputed opinion."[17] Furthermore, the court opinion noted that Congress had sanctioned the establishment of the Commission and the development of commercial nuclear power, and Congress was constitutionally responsible for oversight of Commission regulations and activities. The court showed deference not only to the Commission but also to Congressional policymaking:

It may often be shaky business to attribute significance to the inaction of Congress, but under these circumstances, and considering especially the peculiar responsibility and place of the Joint Committee on Atomic Energy in the statutory scheme, we think it fair to read this history as a de facto acquiescence in and ratification of the Commission's licensing procedure by Congress.[18]

The 1961 precedent of judicial deference to the Commission has been upheld in the final appeal of the majority of cases concerning nuclear power. This deference to the regulatory agency for nuclear power is typical of the judicial review of other administrative agencies. As Martin Shapiro noted in 1968, "At least during the last twenty years the federal court system has devoted the vast bulk of its energies to simply giving legal approval to agency decisions."[19] Ratification of agency rulings is not surprising in view of the fact that the courts are "faced with the same questions of agency policy and power as the agency itself, using roughly the same decisional methods and exposed to roughly the same data."[20] Therefore, when environmentalists have contested Commission safety standards in court, the judiciary has usually declined to overrule the Commission.

Much environmental litigation has concerned Commission regulations for the emergency core cooling system (ECCS), the safety system established to avoid losing the coolant that surrounds the reactor core. The litigation was prompted by the Commission rulemaking proceeding on the ECCS which lasted from January, 1972 until July, 1973, and eventually resulted in the establishment of new safety standards.[21] After these standards were announced, environmentalists charged that they were also inadequate. The first ECCS suit was *Nader* v. *Ray*,[22] asking that a district court issue an injunction to halt nuclear plant operations and revoke the licenses of existing plants. The court did not agree, however, that their continued operation constituted a violation of Commission regulations or that the court had the right to make such a determination prior to the exhaustion of administrative remedies. A similar judicial ruling was issued in another ECCS suit shortly thereafter: *UCS* v. *AEC*.[23] Consequently, Nader, the plaintiff in the original case, went back to the Commission for the new ECCS regulations which the Commission refused to order. Nader contended that the refusal was given "arbitrarily and irrationally," thereby violating the Administrative Procedure Act; and he again took the matter to court in *Nader* v. *NRC*.[24] It was the court of appeals this time that ruled that the NRC's regulations were not arbitrary because they were based on expert opinion.

A second safety consideration that has been brought before the courts by environmental groups is the Commission's siting policy. In the early *Power Reactor Development Co.* v. *International Union of Electric, Radio and Machine Workers*[25] suit in 1961, the siting of a nuclear plant near the population center of Detroit was questioned by the labor union. The

Supreme Court ruled that the Commission had to make its own evaluation of safety considerations regarding plant siting. This court deference to the Commission's authority over site decisions was reiterated in *Porter County Chapter of the Izaak Walton League, Inc.* v. *AEC.*[26] The environmentalists contended that the choice of a plant site in the resort area of the Indiana sand dunes and near the population center of Chicago violated Commission regulations. The court of appeals ruled in favor of the Izaak Walton League; but the Supreme Court overturned the ruling, remanding the case back to the lower court where the construction permit was left intact. In a third and similar case, environmentalists sued the Commission for issuance of a construction permit to build a nuclear plant on a geologic fault: *North Anna Environmental Coalition* v. *NRC.*[27] The court ruled that the Commission had investigated the possibility of seismic activity and determined that the fault was not capable. Consequently, the Commission's site decision was ruled by the court to be within its statutory responsibility to protect public safety.

Another safety matter that has been a frequent subject for litigation is the level of radiation emission standards for nuclear plants. Environmental groups have periodically charged that the Commission standards are not strict enough for the protection of public health and safety. One such case was heard in 1970: *Crowther* v. *Seaborg,*[28] but the court ruled in favor of the Commission's standards. In 1975, environmentalists charged that the Commission was failing to comply with its own regulations concerning radiation levels. In *York Committee for a Safe Environment* v. *NRC,*[29] the plaintiffs objected to numerical standards for radioactive effluents. The Commission's regulations then stated that the level should be "as low as practicable" which, the plaintiffs charged, would make the level vary from one plant to another, depending on the situation. In this case the court agreed that the universal numerical standards should be particularized for each plant and determined on an individual basis. However, since the court found the current level of emissions to be low at the plant then under review, its operating license was not suspended while the Commission analyzed the emission standards on a remand from the court.

There have also been large numbers of court cases brought by antinuclear groups which have attempted to limit the Commission's jurisdiction and transfer some aspect of nuclear power regulation to the states. However, the courts have consistently reaffirmed federal control over radiation standards, citing the "supremacy clause" of the Constitution (Article VI, 2). It says in part: "This Constitution, and the Laws of the United States. . . shall be the supreme Law of the Land . . . . " The courts have held that when Congress has demonstrated its intention, through legislation, to wholly occupy a regulatory field, then state legislation is invalid.

In the landmark federal preemption case *Northern States Power Com-*

pany v. *The State of Minnesota,*[30] the Pollution Control Agency of Minnesota attempted to set more stringent standards regarding radioactive emission from a nuclear plant then under construction than had been set by the Commission. When the utility contested the state standards in court, the court ruled that the Atomic Energy Act of 1954 demonstrated that Congress intended for the Commission to have full power over radioactive emissions: " . . . the federal government has exclusive authority under the doctrine of preemption to regulate the construction and operation of nuclear power plants, which necessarily includes regulation of the levels of radioactive effluents discharged from the plants."[31] The three courts which heard the case: the district court, the court of appeals, and finally the Supreme Court, all agreed that the Commission should have exclusive control over radiation levels.

Although the courts have consistently reaffirmed Commission radiation standards, other areas of the nuclear plant licensing process traditionally fall under state control. The Atomic Energy Act amendment of 1970 says, "Nothing in this section shall be construed to affect the authority of any State or local agency to regulate activities for purposes other than protection against radiation hazards." State regulation may extend to site approval, rate setting, water allocation and other nonradiological matters. The line of demarcation between federal and state authority regarding nuclear plants is hazy, however, and courts are frequently asked to rule on the subject. If the state and federal regulations conflict, the judiciary has usually invoked the preemption doctrine to overrule state authority. For instance, a nuclear plant in New Jersey shut down and, in so doing, lowered the temperature of a nearby creek and brought about the death of a large number of fish. The New Jersey Supreme Court invoked the preemption doctrine to rule that the state could not fine the utility that owned the plant: *State of New Jersery, Department of Environmental Protection* v. *Jersey Central Power and Light Co.*[32] It is entirely possible that the preemption doctrine may also be used to invalidate legislation resulting from the passage of antinuclear state referenda,[33] and it can potentially be used to overturn the restrictive state legislation that has already been enacted, especially in California.[34]

Finally, there have been many suits filed against the Commission contending that its regulatory process does not comply with Congressional statutes. For instance, in *Siegel* v. *AEC,*[35] environmentalists charged that the Commission licensing procedure for a nuclear plant did not protect public safety according to the dictates of the Atomic Energy Act because it failed to investigate the possible dangers of enemy action or terrorist sabotage of the plant. The court of appeals held that the Commission was expected to deal only with the possibility of industrial accidents, not military or terrorist actions, in its hearings process at that time.

The environmentalists have also charged the Commission with failure to comply with the Federal Water Pollution Control Act. This Congressional statute gives the Environmental Protection Agency (EPA) control over discharges into navigable waters. Since the antinuclear groups consider the EPA to be more attuned to environmental concerns than the Commission,[36] they brought suit to transfer control over nuclear plant discharges to the EPA in *Colorado Public Interest Research Group, Inc.* v. *Train.*[37] After conflicting opinions from the district court and the court of appeals, the Supreme Court unanimously agreed to leave the regulation of radioactive materials in the hands of the Commission. The statutory jurisdictional conflict between the Commission and the EPA has remained, however, requiring further Congressional legislation. The recent amendments to the Clean Air Act (August, 1977) have specifically given the EPA control over regulation of radioactive air pollution, which is a legislative victory for the environmental groups.

The litigation with which the environmentalists have been most successful in court suits has been based on the charge that the Commission has failed to comply with the National Environmental Policy Act (NEPA). Although NEPA contained no provision for judicial review, it has become the statutory basis for hundreds of environmental lawsuits. There were more than 400 NEPA lawsuits in the first six years after its enactment.[38] The NEPA mandate for agency consideration of the environmental impact of their projects meant that public interest groups could contest in court the agencies' failure to give the environment sufficient consideration. Antinuclear groups, therefore, filed NEPA–based suits against the Commission although at first it was not clear whether the bill expected that agency licensing proceedings would be viewed as "major Federal action(s)."[39]

In the 1960s environmental groups had begun to charge the Commission with responsibility for controlling the heat discharge from the cooling systems of nuclear plants so that the balance of the ecosystem in lakes, rivers, and coastal waters would not be altered. The Commission, however, refused to assume responsibility for regulation of thermal discharges on the grounds that its Congressional mandate included only the protection of public health and safety. The Supreme Court affirmed the Commission's interpretation of its mandate in *New Hampshire* v. *AEC.*[40] The passage of NEPA did not originally change the Commission's interpretation of its lack of authority over thermal discharges, especially in regard to plants licensed prior to the Act's passage.

The reversal of Commission policy was accomplished by a court opinion handed down in 1971 in *Calvert Cliffs Coordinating Committee* v. *AEC.*[41] It involved an environmental group's suit against the Commission for failure to comply with the Administrative Procedure Act by showing inadequate response to NEPA. The part of NEPA that was ruled to be applicable to the Commission was Section 102 (c) which says:

> All agencies of the Federal Government shall . . . (c) include in every
> recommendation or report on proposals for legislation and other major
> Federal actions significantly affecting the quality of the human environ-
> ment, a detailed statement by the responsible official on (i) the environ-
> mental impact of the proposed action, (ii) any adverse environmental
> effects which cannot be avoided should the proposal be implemented, (iii)
> alternatives to the proposed action, (iv) the relationship between local
> short-term uses of man's environment and the maintenance and enhance-
> ment of long-term productivity, and (v) any irreversible and irretrievable
> commitments of resources which would be involved in the proposed action
> should it be implemented.

Specifically, the Calvert Cliffs case concerned an environmental
group's efforts to force the Commission to halt construction of a nuclear
plant on Maryland's Chesapeake Bay. The plaintiffs charged that the Commission's licensing procedure violated NEPA because an environmental
impact statement (EIS) had not been prepared for the plant; and nor had
the Commission made an independent assessment of such environmental
concerns as water quality, having relied on reports from other agencies. The
court of appeals strongly agreed with the plaintiffs regarding the Commission's lack of compliance with NEPA. In fact, the Calvert Cliffs opinion
shows considerable annoyance with the Commission and is highly critical of
the nuclear plant licensing process, using such words as "crabbed,"
"shocking," "ludicrous," "total abdication," and "pointless."

The court ruled that construction of Calvert Cliffs and all nuclear
plants would have to be halted while an EIS was prepared for each of them.
The Commission was directed to make an independent evaluation for each
plant of the environmental costs of the plant's construction without relying
on opinions from other agencies. Then the Commission was to counterbal-
ance those costs against the technical and economic benefits that each plant
would provide:

> NEPA mandates a case-by-case balancing judgment on the part of federal
> agencies. In each individual case, the particular economic and technical
> benefits of planned action must be assessed and then weighed against the
> environmental costs; alternatives must be considered which would affect
> the balance of values . . . .[42]

The effect of the Calvert Cliffs decision was far reaching, certainly
more so than any other court opinion in regard to nuclear plants. Since the
Commission had exempted from the need for environmental impact statements the nuclear plants that had applied for a construction permit before
March 4, 1971, the court opinion overruled that exemption. Therefore, the

five plants that were already operating and the seven that were engaged in hearings for operating licenses were retroactively affected.[43] There was an eighteen month halt in the licensing process while the Commission made its independent environmental evaluations and issued an EIS for each plant. Because Congress was concerned about the loss of electricity from the nuclear plants during the court-ordered delay in operation, special legislation was enacted to authorize Commission issuance of interim licenses that allowed the plants to continue construction and to operate at partial capacity while an EIS was being prepared.[44] The Commission initially intended to appeal the Calvert Cliffs ruling, but James Schlesinger replaced Glenn Seaborg as the Commission chairman and announced on August 26, 1971, that there would be no appeal.[45]

NEPA, and its interpretation by the court in Calvert Cliffs, started a rash of litigation by public interest groups. *Scientists' Institute for Public Information, Inc.* v. *AEC*[46] was heard shortly after Calvert Cliffs and concerned an appropriations request for a breeder reactor, rather than the light water reactor. However, the significance of its opinion extended to both types of nuclear power in that the court ruled that the Commission was obligated to make reasonable forecasts of future environmental impact to the extent of its current technical knowledge in order to comply with NEPA.

Many of the NEPA suits have concerned the requirement that agencies must balance environmental costs against a project's benefits. Not only in the Calvert Cliffs case, but also in *Crowther* v. *Seaborg*[47] and *Citizens for Safe Power, Inc.* v. *NRC,*[48] the courts have specifically authorized the Commission to weigh the risks against the advantages of atomic energy. However, the Commission has avoided consideration in the licensing process of the so-called Class 9 catastrophic accidents.[49] The probability of the occurrence of Class 9 accidents is deemed by the Commission to be too small to merit its consideration. The court of appeals upheld this view in *Carolina Environmental Study Group* v. *U.S.,*[50] saying that NEPA did not require Commission study of "every extreme possibility which might be conjectured."[51]

The Carolina Environmental Study Group had also charged that the Commission violated NEPA by failing to consider alternatives to the proposed plant, such as oil shale, geothermal, solar energy, or energy conservation. The court ruled, however, that the Commission was expected to examine "alternatives as they exist and are likely to exist,"[52] not to study technologies not yet fully available. It may be concluded, therefore, that the courts "will generally treat requests for EIS preparation sympathetically,"[53] as in Calvert Cliffs; but when an EIS is prepared, the courts do not insist that it deal with every conceivable alternative to the proposed project or risk involved in the project.

Thus, the judiciary has generally upheld the Commission's interpretation of its own regulations and safety standards concerning siting, the emergency core cooling system, and radioactive emission levels. The judges have cited the preemption doctrine to prevent state legislative incursion into the Commission's field of regulation of radiation standards. In addition, the courts have exercised judicial restraint in regard to the interpretation of Congressional statutes, except in the Calvert Cliffs opinion on the National Environmental Policy Act. In other cases, the judiciary has acquiesced to the Commission's exclusion of improbable risks and currently unavailable technologies from consideration in the environmental impact statements of nuclear plants. With the exception of Calvert Cliffs, then, the antinuclear groups have been generally unsuccessful at obtaining judicial endorsement of their concerns.

Overview of the Impact of Legal Advocacy

It would seem that the interest group that most frequently benefited from judicial rulings would be the one that most often initiated litigation. As Jack Peltason phrased it, "Groups which judges support support judges."[54] However, in regard to atomic energy lawsuits, just the opposite has been true. The majority of judicial rulings have favored the nuclear industry position, but the industry has rarely initiated lawsuits itself. In fact, every single one of the major, precedent–setting suits regarding nuclear power policy has been filed by the antinuclear environmental groups, with the single exception of *Northern States Power Company* v. *State of Minnesota.*[55] Furthermore, in the Northern States case, the utility did not take advantage of its judicial victory.[56]

Besides avoiding the initiation of court suits, the nuclear industry has sometimes refrained from appealing the judicial rulings that have been made against it by the lower courts. For example, the judicial opinion that had the most detrimental consequences on the development of nuclear power was *Calvert Cliffs Coordinating Committee* v. *AEC.*[57] By requiring an environmental impact statement for each proposed atomic plant, the court opinion initially stopped the licensing of all plants for an 18–month period. It retroactively affected twelve plants and greatly increased the scope and complexity of the licensing process for all future nuclear plants. Although it is generally agreed that an appeal of the Calvert Cliffs ruling would probably not have reversed the court of appeals decision, the Supreme Court might have overruled its retroactive provisions or provided the Commission with clearer procedural guidelines for future plant licensing, thereby making the legal ramifications of the Commission's licensing decisions more certain. The antinuclear groups had expected that the nuclear industry would appeal the Calvert Cliffs ruling,[58] but no petition for *certiorari* was filed either by the Commission or by the utilities.

The frequent judicial review of Commission decisions has probably affected the agency's performance of its regulatory and licensing functions. In fact, the members of the Commission have often commented that their work is done in a "fishbowl,"[59] in part because of all the litigation. Daniel Fiorino, an observer of the interrelationship between the regulatory agencies and the courts, has noted that most agency personnel try to make policy decisions that "anticipate and overcome possible objections from the courts."[60] Therefore, it is likely that the Commission strives to follow proper procedures to the letter so that the judiciary will not overturn its decisions on procedural grounds.

However, the Commission is often uncertain about what constitutes a proper procedure. The statutory language in such legislation as the National Environmental Policy Act, for example, is very ambiguous and may be interpreted in a number of ways. Experience has shown the Commission that the intervenors are likely to file a suit against it when it does not accede to their statutory interpretations regarding procedures. On the other hand, the Commission must also realize that denial of the nuclear industry's procedural requests is unlikely to result in the industry's initiation of judicial review of the Commission's decisions. Therefore, it is likely that the Commission is more careful to comply with the intervenors' procedural interpretations than with those of the nuclear industry because the Commission naturally prefers to avoid possible judicial remands. To the dismay of the nuclear industry, the duration of the Commission's proceedings is usually extended by acquiescing to the intervenors' interpretations, and the proceedings become more lengthy than the statutory mandate would necessarily oblige them to be. Thus, the one-sided use of legal advocacy by environmental groups has probably made the Commission's procedural decisions more sympathetic to the antinuclear groups' requests and has extended the duration of the Commission's regulatory and licensing process.

An additional advantage to the environmental groups' initiation of litigation is the fact that their position as the aggrieved party has given them the right to choose the court in which a suit will be filed. When the Commission's issuance of a nuclear power plant license is appealed, the suit may be heard either in the local court of appeals or in the Court of Appeals for the District of Columbia Circuit. Each of the eleven federal courts of appeals is characterized by reputations regarding their judicial attitudes. For example, the District of Columbia Circuit is considered to be a liberal court that sympathizes with environmental and consumer groups, while the Fourth Circuit is known to be more favorably inclined toward industry.[61] Furthermore, it is often unwise for environmental groups to bring suits against major projects in the court serving the area that will benefit economically from the project.[62]

Consequently, wise litigants study the reputation of their local federal court to decide whether it is more advantageous to file the suit there or to file it in the Court of Appeals for the D.C. Circuit. When both parties to a case want to file a suit, they are apt to differ on their choice of appellate court. As a result, there are often regulatory rulings, from agencies other than the Nuclear Regulatory Commission, which precipitate an actual race among the groups affected by the decision to determine which will institute the first appeal, thereby selecting the court most likely to return a favorable judgment.[63] In the case of nuclear licensing decisions, there has never been a race of this kind because it has only been the environmental groups that have appealed the regulatory rulings. Their exclusive use of legal advocacy has given them the undisputed right to the choice of the court that would potentially be most sympathetic to their lawsuits.

For the antinuclear groups, the most beneficial feature of the judicial process has been its duration. The fact that these groups have usually been granted standing has made it possible for them to secure judicial review of nuclear power cases without difficulty and then extend the litigation process through appeals. For example, *Northern States Power Co.* v. *Minnesota*[64] was involved in adjudication in the District Court for the District of Minnesota, then the 8th Circuit Court of Appeals and, finally, the Supreme Court, from August, 1969 until April, 1972. The case of *Porter County Chapter of the Izaak Walton League* v. *AEC*[65] was argued in December, 1974, in the 7th Circuit Court of Appeals and decided in April, 1975; heard by the Supreme Court and remanded in November, 1975; heard again in the 7th Circuit Court in April, 1976; and denied a rehearing by that court in June, 1976; and then denied certiorari by the Supreme Court in November, 1976. In both cases, the judiciary ruled in favor of the Commission, but the judicial delays slowed the construction of the atomic plants and had a demoralizing effect on the nuclear industry.

Antinuclear groups have taken advantage of judicial delays to bolster their resolve and resources, as well as to educate the public and mobilize opposition to the plants. However, an even greater benefit derived by the environmental groups from court-ordered injunctions is the expense of the delay for the utilities that have ordered or built the plants. There are three ways in which prolongation of a plant's construction schedule increases the plant's construction costs: first, the utility must pay additional interest charges on any money it has borrowed to finance the construction; second, inflation drives up the cost of purchasing labor and equipment at a date later than originally anticipated;[66] and, third, with frequent revisions and updating of regulatory requirements, prolongation of the time frame for a plant's construction necessitates design changes that entail additional expense. Furthermore, the utility must often satisfy its electric customers' demands with electricity purchased at higher prices from adjoining power companies, or else it must construct additional fossil fuel plants itself to fill the void while the nuclear plant's construction is being delayed.

When a nuclear plant is ready for operation but lies idle waiting for the resolution of a court suit, the expense to a utility is even greater than that incurred during a construction delay. Former Energy Secretary Schlesinger estimated that each year a typical plant's operation was postponed cost the utility about $120 million.[67] When a utility experiences economic setbacks of this magnitude because of litigation involving its nuclear plant, the result is frequently a decision on the part of the utility not to commit itself to atomic plants in the future.

The enormity of the effect of delay on the utilities may best be demonstrated by their acceptance of out-of-court settlements to avoid the economic risk inherent in the litigation process. For example, environmentalists used the threat of continued regulatory and judicial delays to force Consumers Power Company to install $28 million worth of added environmental safeguards beyond the Commission's requirements at its Palisades nuclear plant. The 9 months of postponement of the plant's operation already caused by the intervenors had cost Consumers Power $1 million per month, plus the added cost of buying power from other utilities.[68] Similarly, Florida Power and Light Company agreed to install a cooling system on a nuclear plant, and Commonwealth Edison decreased a plant's radioactive emission level in return for promises from environmental groups not to delay the plant's licensing.[69] In these cases, as well, environmental groups were also employing the possibility of regulatory and judicial stalling to force costly concessions from the utilities that went beyond Commission standards. The utilities were not apprehensive about the outcome of the court cases, only about the lengthy litigation process. The duration of the judicial process had made it a no-lose tactic for nuclear power opponents.

Summary and Conclusions

The fact that almost all the major court suits regarding nuclear power policy have been initiated by the environmentalists has brought them the prerogative of choosing the most sympathetic court as the one in which a case will be heard. Nonetheless, the content of the policy output from the judicial process has generally favored the nuclear industry. In the majority of cases, the courts have upheld the Commission's rulings regarding nuclear plant regulations and safety standards, and the judicial affirmation of the preemption doctrine has allowed the Commission's radiation standards to supersede those of the states. Although the courts have usually restrained themselves from involvement in the Commission's interpretation of Congressional statutes, the Calvert Cliffs case is an important exception to that generalization.

In spite of the many judicial rulings favorable to the nuclear industry, the judicial process has had a very detrimental policy impact in regard to the development of nuclear power. By extending the licensing process with lengthy litigation, the environmental groups have added substantial costs to plants whose construction period is extended or whose operation is delayed pending a court decision. The nuclear industry has been demoralized by the threat and use of legal advocacy and has sometimes accepted expensive out-of-court settlements to avoid further adjudicatory delay. Thus, the content of the judicial output of rulings favorable to the nuclear industry has been superseded by the impact of the duration of the judicial process. The case study of the Midland nuclear plant will illustrate this phenomenon.

5 The Interest Groups at Midland

This chapter begins a case study of the Midland nuclear plant licensing process. It presents a comparison of the antinuclear environmental groups opposing the Midland nuclear power plant and the nuclear industry promoting it, just as chapter 2 analyzed the characteristics of the pro- and antinuclear groups at the national level. The same measures will be examined: the degree and appropriateness of the groups' organization (ideological motivations, organizational framework, and cohesion); their organizational resources (funds, leadership skills, and coalitions with other groups); and, finally, their choice of strategies. The Commission's rulings in regard to the Midland construction permit hearings will also be described, as well as the effect of that decision on the interest groups prior to the start of litigation.

Background of the Midland Controversy

The nuclear controversy in Midland was triggered by the announcement on December 14, 1967, that an atomic power plant would be built nearby. Consumers Power Company, a utility headquartered in Jackson, Michigan, publicized its plans to construct a plant with two pressurized light-water reactors on a 650-acre site on the southern shore of the Tittabawassee River. That site is located in Midland, a central Michigan city of 35,000 residents located 200 miles northwest of Detroit. Consumers Power announced that the plant would generate 1.3 million kilowatts for the statewide electric system. In addition, it would deliver over 4 million pounds of process steam per hour for industrial and heating use by Dow Chemical Company, located just across the river from the site chosen for the nuclear plant. Dow Chemical Company is the largest user of process steam in the country. The proposed Midland plant was to be one of the world's largest dual purpose facilities, using the process known as cogeneration to produce both steam and electricity. The two units of the plant were slated for completion in 1974 and 1975, at a projected cost of $349 million.

As was explained in chapter 3, there is an elaborate two-step administrative process involved in the licensing of a nuclear power plant. Consumers Power Company filed its application for a construction permit for the Midland plant with the Commission on January 13, 1969. After the Commission staff and the Advisory Committee on Reactor Safeguards (ACRS) evaluated the application, it was submitted to the Atomic Safety and Licensing Board (ASLB) for a decision. The ASLB conducted public hearings on the construction permit application so that outside individuals and groups could present their concerns. These hearings began on December 1, 1970. There were several parties directly involved at the time, most of whom remained involved throughout the hearings and subsequent court appeals. Consumers Power Company and the Dow Chemical Company were the parties supporting the application. The intervenors opposing the construction permit were divided into two groups: one, hereafter referred to as the Saginaw Intervenors, consisted of a coalition of the Saginaw Valley Nuclear Study Group, the United Auto Workers International, the Citizens Committee for Environmental Protection of Michigan, West Michigan Environmental Action Council, Inc., Sierra Club and University of Michigan Environmental Law Society; the other was composed only of the Mapleton Intervenors.

The Antinuclear Groups at Midland

The antinuclear environmental groups at Midland shared the same motivating perceptions. As on the national level, the antinuclear forces at the Midland hearings were comprised of citizen groups or public interest groups. Their organizational incentives were ideological, and they sought what they perceived to be the collective good. They shared a common concern about the safety of the proposed nuclear plant and its effect on the health of the local populace. They raised literally hundreds of safety questions at the ASLB hearings, the same types of questions posed by other antinuclear groups across the country. Prominent among the safety questions they raised was the Saginaw Intervenors' criticism of the proximity of the plant to the Dow chemical complex and to the town of Midland, the downtown area of which was within two miles of the plant site. The Mapleton Intervenors especially concentrated their efforts on discussion of the fog and icing hazards that could potentially be caused by the plant's 880–acre cooling pond.

According to Mary Sinclair, the intervenors' leader, they did not originally oppose construction of the plant. They intended to use the forum provided by the intervention in the public hearings to ask questions to ensure that the plant, when built, would be as safe as possible.[1] It was only as the hearings progressed that there was a growing conviction among all the intervenor groups that a nuclear plant should not be constructed at all.

The antinuclear commitment of the intervenors in the Midland hearings was reinforced by attitudes shared with the national environmental groups. Firstly, there was a feeling of preference for a no–risk environment, as well as distrust of the scientific community, especially the Commission, which might overlook questions of public health and safety. Secondly, the intervenors favored maintenance of the status quo in Midland, a no-growth philosophy because " . . . their life styles, their occupations, and their investments, both emotional and financial, will be threatened by the construction and operation of the proposed plants."[2] Thirdly, the antinuclear groups at Midland shared the motivation of other groups in that they disliked high degrees of economic centralization and were wary of "the corporations, commercial organizations, and government agencies who developed powerful vested interest in certain decisions."[3]

The Saginaw Valley Nuclear Study Group presented the major opposition to the nuclear plant in the administrative hearings process. As the leadership group, it provided a cohesive, well-defined organizational framework for the intervenors. It was a local group headquartered in the city of Midland and organized by Mary Sinclair, a Midland resident. Her role as wife of one of Midland's attorneys and the mother of five lent respectability to the group she led. For instance, she was featured in a flattering society page article in the Sunday *Bay City Times*.[4] Her background as a technical writer and researcher added credibility to her skepticism about the safety of atomic energy. She wrote a fifty-six page booklet called *Nuclear Power and Public Concern,* and several thousand copies were distributed.

In examining the antinuclear environmental groups in chapter 2, the conclusion was reached that one of their most important organizational resources is effective leadership. The same can be said for the intervenor groups at Midland. From the beginning, Mary Sinclair exhibited relentless dedication to her cause. She read with care every available bit of information from the Commission and the utility, educating herself and looking for safety issues to question during the hearings. She raised funds herself through lectures, classes and solicitations of support for the Saginaw Intervenors. Equally important, she tried to compensate for the small number of local people in the group through persistent activism in public meetings, frequent communications with government officials, and procurement of much media coverage. Furthermore, her organizational ability can be credited with the involvement of the other five groups that joined in forming the Saginaw Intervenors;[5] and her leadership extended not only to the Saginaw groups but also to the Citizens Committee for Environmental Protection of Michigan, of which she was president, and the Consolidated National Intervenors, a national coalition of sixty environmental groups, of which she was codirector.

The Saginaw Valley Nuclear Study Group held its first organizing meeting on October 7, 1970, at a local church. The group's membership was open to all interested citizens, and it continued to extend open invitations to the public to attend its meetings. However, at its peak, the group only consisted of about thirty members. The members of the group were mostly the representatives from the affiliated intervenor organizations that were particularly concerned about the Midland plant. They held numerous forums to educate the public about the potential dangers of nuclear power, and they took every opportunity to speak to local groups and gain media coverage. It was the Saginaw organization that initially made the decision to intervene in the licensing hearings, and it was Mary Sinclair herself who made the decision to hire lawyer Myron Cherry to represent the group. Her leadership of the Saginaw group typified the personalized decision making that occurs in many of the national environmental groups.

The Saginaw group was also characteristic of most antinuclear groups in maximizing its strength through the development of coalitions among disparate groups. The other five organizations that lent their name to the intervention effort included the Sierra Club. Largely responsible for its involvement was Kathleen Bjerke, an activist in the Saginaw Valley Nuclear Study Group who also served as chairperson of the conservation committee of the Mackinac chapter of the Sierra Club, as well as on its Executive Committee. The Sierra Club's particular concern with the nuclear plant, in addition to safety questions, was the projected population growth and industrial expansion that the plant was apt to cause in the Tri–City area. Although the national Sierra Club had not formally expressed a position regarding the development of nuclear power in 1970, there was apprehension among some of the Club's leaders about atomic power as an energy source. Consequently, the local chapter could rely on the national organization for much of its funding.

A second organization that was drawn into the intervenor group through overlapping memberships was the West Michigan Environmental Action Council since some of its officers were members of the Sierra Club. The Council was located in Grand Rapids. It was part of a coalition of fifty organizations and had a number of individual members. Like the Sierra Club and the Saginaw Valley Nuclear Study Group, the West Michigan Environmental Action Council originally had taken no formal stand against nuclear power in general or the Midland plant in particular but joined the intervenors to help ensure that the plant would be built as safely as possible. It was not until 1971 that Peter Steketee, the group's leader, announced that his position had changed to complete opposition to the plant's construction.[6]

The intervention of the United Auto Workers in the Midland hearings was motivated from the beginning by its opposition to nuclear power plants. The UAW prides itself on its involvement in social issues, saying " . . . our concern is for the general public as well as our members in the misuse of our natural resources."[7] In 1971 a Michigan UAW Community Action Program resolution called for a general moratorium on the building of nuclear power plants. The union's opposition to atomic energy in the early 1970s had been sparked by the personal conviction of UAW President Walter Reuther. His influence resulted in UAW involvement at the Fermi I and Palisades plants' licensing hearings in Michigan, as well as at other hearings across the country.[8] Consequently, UAW affiliation with the Saginaw Intervenors was an outgrowth of its general policies. Its contribution to the intervenors was not only its name but also a "few hundred dollars."[9]

The other two groups affiliated with the Saginaw Intervenors were the Citizens Committee for Environmental Protection of Michigan and the University of Michigan Environmental Law Society. The Citizens Committee was the first environmental group that Mary Sinclair had organized, and it was made up of local residents especially concerned with safety issues. The University of Michigan Law School students had joined forces with the intervenors " . . . to demonstrate to the people of the United States and Michigan, particularly the young activist community, that environmental protection can be achieved through established administrative and legal channels."[10] These law students contributed some *pro bono* legal work to the Midland case.

The coalition of six groups called the Saginaw Intervenors was joined in the licensing hearings by a separate group called the Mapleton Intervenors. It consisted of eight homeowners and businessmen from the small community of Mapleton, just one mile from the proposed plant site. They were led by Wendall Marshall whose concern with the nuclear plant was less the safety question at first than the nuisance it might cause and the effect it would have on property values. The Mapleton Intervenors did not schedule public meetings and educational talks on the effects of nuclear power as the Saginaw Intervenors did. Although the Saginaw group was eager to generate as broad a base of antinuclear support as possible, it declined to consolidate with the Mapleton Intervenors, even when asked to do so, because, as Mary Sinclair expressed it, " . . . we have national groups and we have a broader range and issues."[11] The basic cohesion of the two intervenor groups may best be described, however, by noting that their attorneys shared documents during the licensing hearings.

In addition to the groups already mentioned, there were other organizations interested in participation in the intervention. The Environmental Defense Fund (EDF), a national public interest group oriented toward the use of legal advocacy, initially filed its own petition to intervene in the Midland hearings. The EDF's particular concerns were compliance with the National Environmental Policy Act at Midland and assurance of the safety of the emergency core cooling system. These issues were eventually dealt with in other forums, so it is not surprising that Anthony Roisman, the EDF attorney, petitioned the Commission to withdraw from the Midland hearings in May, 1972, prior to their completion.

As the EDF prematurely withdrew, so the state of Kansas belatedly joined the intervention. Its motivation may best be explained by its petition to the Commission:

> Because it is contemplated by the Atomic Energy Commission that the Lyons, Kansas, facility will be the nuclear waste repository for the foreseeable future, wastes inevitably created by the operation of the Consumers Power Company Midland plant may be unavoidably committed to transportation and disposal in Kansas, involving a potential threat to the lives, health and well–being of Kansas.[12]

Other groups, such as the local chapter of Trout, Unlimited, considered joining the intervenors but eventually decided not to do so. In addition, the Saginaw Intervenors had the financial and/or moral support of a variety of local and national organizations.[13] The Audubon Society which, along with the Sierra Club, offered its name for tax–deductible contributions to the Saginaw Intervenors, also furnished them with technical information.

Thanks to the energetic leadership of Mary Sinclair and others, as well as the support of broad coalitions, the Midland intervenor groups were able to raise money for their attorneys. The Saginaw Intervenors paid Myron Cherry more than $100,000.[14] The funds came from individuals, sympathetic local and national antinuclear groups, and foundations. There were times during the regulatory hearings and subsequent litigation when the intervenors considered withdrawing due to lack of sufficient funds, but financial constraints actually caused nonparticipation only in the show-cause hearing regarding quality assurance violations in 1974.[15]

Though the help of attorneys is costly, all the parties at nuclear plant licensing hearings (the intervenors, the nuclear industry and the Commission) are usually represented by lawyers. As mentioned previously, it was Mary Sinclair who chose Myron Cherry to represent the Saginaw Intervenors in the Midland licensing hearings. She chose him, she said, because he is "bright, dedicated and mean."[16] Most observers reiterate this double-edged description of Cherry as both capable and abrasive in his courtroom manner. He is able to dominate any proceedings in which he takes part. Cherry is a Chicago lawyer who had represented the intervenors in the operating license hearings for Consumers Power Company's Palisades nuclear power plant in 1970. He had eventually forced Consumers Power to install $28 million worth of cooling towers and other environmental safeguards at the plant in an out-of-court settlement in which he agreed not to engage the utility in further court action. Thanks to the Palisades hearings, Cherry quickly developed a national reputation, serving as the chief attorney for the Consolidated National Intervenors at the emergency core cooling system (ECCS) rulemaking hearings, as well as for other environmental groups such as the Friends of the Earth.

In selecting Cherry to represent them, the Saginaw Intervenors were also committing themselves to the strategy of delay; Cherry's trademark as a successful antinuclear lawyer has been his skill at prolonging the hearings and litigation process. In his initial efforts at Palisades, Cherry took pride in using cross-examination to extend the hearings for more than nine months.[17] Cherry correctly observed that dilatory tactics made the commitment to the nuclear power plant "as painful and expensive as possible for a utility."[18] Ralph Nader's recent book on nuclear power notes a further advantage of using such tactics: "Chicago attorney Myron Cherry, who has represented several intervenors, believes that the intervention process can delay licensing and allow public opposition to the plant to develop further."[19]

Cherry's use of dilatory tactics contributed to the duration of the Midland hearings for the initial construction permit licensing process from December 1, 1970, until December 15, 1972. He requested a series of postponements of the ASLB hearings, explaining that he required time to formulate his case against the plant. At one point, he said that he especially needed a postponement because he was participating in eleven other cases that also took his time, and furthermore, his assistant in the Midland case was a Purdue student whose "academic schedule does not permit him to assist me" until later in the year.[20]

Cherry used the Midland construction permit hearings to question every aspect of the national development of commercial nuclear power. Accordingly, he submitted over 300 interrogatories (written questions) to the Commission at the hearings; and it took additional time for Consumers Power, Dow, and the Midland Nuclear Power Committee, to whom the questions were directed, to provide replies. There were eventually more than 9000 pages of testimony before the ASLB. The public hearings process lasted for two years during which time construction activity and design engineering for the project were halted. Construction was delayed from November, 1970 until June, 1973. By the time the construction and engineering were resumed, the projected cost of the Midland plant had nearly doubled. Cherry made delay a substantive issue as well as a procedural one.

Cherry was initially joined in his efforts on behalf of the Saginaw Intervenors by the attorneys for the Mapleton Intervenors, the most effective of whom was Irving Like of New York. Like concurred with Cherry about the value of the Commission hearing as a means for educating the public about the potential dangers of nuclear power and increasing public opposition to a proposed plant. In a law review article entitled "Multi-Media Confrontation—The Environmentalists' Strategy for a 'No-Win' Agency Proceeding," Like stated, " . . . it is the duty of citizen intervenors to transform the agency hearings into a dramatic medium, which by its content and total effect will educate the public and its opinion and policy makers to the possible environmental hazards . . . . ''[21] Accordingly, Like and Cherry both played to media coverage during the hearings process.

The Mapleton group also agreed with Cherry about the value of dilatory tactics, admitting that its goal was delay.[22] The Mapleton Intervenors took six months to file their specific objections to the Midland plant with the ASLB and then prolonged the questioning with what the ASLB chairman termed a verbal ''fishing expedition.''[23] Thus, all the intervenors in the Midland hearings joined forces to extend the licensing process as long as possible. After, the construction permit was finally issued in 1972, Cherry and Like continued their strategy of drawing out the regulatory process by filing an exception to the initial decision in January, 1973, but the Atomic Licensing and Safety Appeal Board confirmed the Midland permit. The intervenors made subsequent appeals to the Commission to revoke the Midland construction permit and/or raise new issues for further examination of the permit on seven different occasions before the Midland case was heard by the Court of Appeals to which they had appealed the Commission's ruling.

The Nuclear Industry at Midland

At the Midland hearings, the nuclear industry was represented by Consumers Power Company, the utility that proposed to build the Midland nuclear plant, and Consumers had the support of Dow Chemical Company which had signed a contract to buy process steam from the plant. The utility's motivations for proposing a nuclear plant mirrored those of the national nuclear industry: it was ''strictly a matter of economics'' since nuclear power seemed to be less expensive than other forms of energy.[24] Consumers Power projected that Michigan's demand for energy would increase to the point where an additional plant would be necessary by the mid-1970s to keep pace with the growth of the state. Furthermore, as the Dow officials repeatedly pointed out, they would not have committed themselves to the development of a nuclear plant in the town where they lived and worked if they were not convinced of its safety.

Consumers Power Company is an investor-owned utility supplying both gas and electricity to a population of over 5 million. Its electric service area includes most of the Lower Peninsula of Michigan outside of Detroit, and the company has about 11,000 employees. Its corporate commitment to the development of atomic energy, along with other energy sources, was evidenced by its Big Rock Point nuclear power plant which went into service in 1962 as the nation's fifth commercial nuclear plant and by the Palisades nuclear plant which started operation in December, 1971, a year after the Midland licensing hearings began. By 1977, nearly 20 percent of the electricity supplied by Consumers Power came from its two atomic plants.

Due to the nature of the Commission's licensing process, it is necessary for a utility to invest millions of dollars in engineering and design manhours in order to have sufficient data on its proposed nuclear plant to submit an application for a construction license. Consequently, Consumer Power had completed half of the plant's engineering design before the ASLB public hearings began in Midland in December, 1970. Furthermore, Consumers Power followed the practice that was then customary of requesting permission from the Commission to proceed at its own risk with site preparation and preconstruction activity in July, 1970.[25] When the ASLB hearings began, therefore, Consumers Power had already excavated the site of its 880–acre cooling pond for the plant. Thus, the utility's investment in the Midland plant was sizable before the environmental groups ever submitted petitions to intervene in hearings to challenge the plant's construction. Consumers Power's ideological and economic commitment to the plant continued to grow as the regulatory and adjudicatory process was extended.

Midland is the home of the world headquarters of the Dow Chemical Company, one of the largest industrial corporations in the United States. Dow Chemical employs about 31,000 American employees, with 7,000 in Midland alone, and its earnings in 1977 were over half a billion dollars. At the time that Dow and Consumers Power agreed on their contract for the Midland plant, it was the largest contract Dow had ever signed. Dow planned to use the Midland nuclear plant to replace its own outdated fossil–fueled plant as the source of its process steam and electricity. Like Consumers Power, Dow's commitment to the nuclear plant became greater during the licensing hearings because its coal plant's life span was ending, and it was becoming subject to pressures from the Environmental Protection Agency and the Michigan State Pollution Control Commission regarding the coal plant's environmental violations. Dow knew that it needed an alternate energy source as soon as possible.

The cohesion of the two companies in the regulatory process was initially very strong. The announcement of the Midland plant in 1967 climaxed a year of negotiations between the two companies, with the size, location, and cost of the proposed plant being affected by Dow's position as its major customer.

In 1974, the two companies signed an additional contract for the purchase of steam from the Midland plant. Throughout the first six years of regulatory hearings, the top officials of Dow and Consumers Power (A.H. Aymond, James Campbell and, later John Selby of Consumers, and Carl Gerstacker, C.B. Branch and, later, Paul Oreffice and David Rooke of Dow Chemical Company) shared a unified public stand and a cohesive organizational framework. Their various attorneys worked together for the development of the Midland plant. It was not until the end of 1976 that the public learned that the years of delay had produced a strain in their relationship.

During the two years of licensing hearings for the Midland plant's construction permit, the strategy of the two companies was to encourage public support for the plant. Consumers Power sent many of its officials, from the president on down, to speak in Midland at the public information meetings and press briefings that it scheduled. Since nuclear power evoked a great deal of curiosity in the community after the plant was proposed, an environmental scientist from the utility was specifically designated to handle the numerous speaking engagements that were requested by clubs, schools, churches, political groups, and other local organizations. In addition, Consumers Power set up a Nuclear Information Center at the plant site that offered tours and answered questions for the thousands of people who filed through it in 1970 and succeeding years.

Equally important, the utility sought to allay the specific concerns of the local citizenry by making improvements in the original plant design. In May, 1971, it unilaterally decided to reduce the release of radioactive wastes in the form of gas from the plant to 6 percent of the allowable limits, saying that it might later be reduced to zero.[26] In July, 1971, the company also decided to build additional facilities at the plant to insure against thermal pollution in the Tittabawassee River.

The Dow Company made similar efforts to overcome concerns about the Midland plant. It explained its own commitment to nuclear power in the company newsletters that were sent to the homes of its thousands of Midland employees. Dow also provided local groups with speakers and utilized other public relations techniques. When a few of its employees joined the environmental groups, Dow temporarily engaged in what the intervenors considered to be corporate harassment.[27]

By far the most public support for the nuclear plant resulted from Dow's decision to make cutbacks in production and jobs in Midland. Before the ASLB public hearings began, Dow explained that refusal to grant a construction permit for the plant could "require Dow to minimize the future role of its Midland plant and to construct chemical plants in other areas of the country and the world where sources of energy, which are economically and environmentally acceptable, are available."[28] As the hearings dragged on for the first half of 1971, Dow officials publicized the fact that the Midland employment level was at a fifteen–year low, which could be corrected by the development of the Midland nuclear plant. A month later the company made a further cutback in the Midland labor force and shut down the propylene oxide plant. Additional cutbacks ensued in succeeding years.

Dow and Consumers Power Company were inundated by public support for the nuclear power plant in Midland. A national survey by Response Analysis Corporation in May, 1971, included a subsample on Midland showing that 85 percent of its people favored the nuclear plant and only 4 percent opposed it.[29] As the local newspaper remarked, "never in the history of Midland or the tri-county area has there been such unanimity on a public issue."[30] All of the local government officials and more than sixty local organizations, from the Midland County Medical Society to the Midland Board of Education, jumped on the bandwagon behind Dow and Consumers Power.[31] The Mayor of Midland went on record saying that the town was "the first community in history to form a citizens group to promote construction of a nuclear power plant."[32]

The motivations of the pronuclear groups were readily apparent. Midland is a company town where, in addition to paying the salaries of as many as half of the working people, Dow has also provided educational and cultural facilities for the people and engendered a feeling of gratitude to the company. Besides wanting to support Dow in its commitment to the nuclear plant, the local residents hoped the town's economy and industry would grow. They saw that the employment level at Dow was falling at the rate of one job per day as the hearings were delayed. Furthermore, when the nuclear plant was under construction, it promised to create 2500 jobs with an annual payroll of $56 million plus nearly double that amount in other service jobs in the community. Finally, the community is largely comprised of highly educated technicians and scientists, most of whom are satisfied with the safety record of atomic power. The prospect of having a nuclear plant that would not create the smog and fly-ash of Dow's coal-fired plant also appealed to the community.

With the support of the Midland Chamber of Commerce, the various pronuclear groups coalesced into the Midland Nuclear Power Committee. It was headed by Dr. Wayne North, pastor of the Methodist Church; and its funds came entirely from small local businesses and individual contributions. The Midland Nuclear Power Committee originally intervened in the ASLB hearings in support of the plant, and it also engaged in other public relations efforts, especially newspaper ads.

As the ASLB hearings dragged on with no construction permit in sight, demonstrations of public support for the plant in the town of Midland were made to try to expedite the hearings process. The Midland Nuclear Power Committee received $20,000 of public funds from the Midland County Board of Commissioners. This money was used to stage a huge pronuclear rally in Midland in October, 1971, which was attended by a crowd of 20,000 and featured speakers urging an end to the licensing hearings. The Midland Nuclear Power Committee also sent letters to government officials asking that the hearings be delayed no longer, and supportive responses were received from Governor William Milliken, Senators Philip Hart and Robert Griffin, and some of the Michigan Congressmen. Furthermore, although the *Bay City Times* questioned the safety of the plant,[33] Midland's local newspaper, the *Midland Daily News,* favored a quicker licensing process and repeatedly criticized the intervenors in editorials for prolonging the hearings "almost indefinitely,"[34] saying "from the beginning the tactic of delay has been in the forefront."[35] The Midland television station WNEM-TV and its radio station WMPX also favored a speedy licensing of the nuclear plant.[36]

Thus, there is no question but what the nuclear industry was effective in its strategy of encouraging public support for the plant. However, the public pressures to expedite the hearings seemed to have no effect on the ASLB. Consumers Power had hired several attorneys, including Robert Lowenstein from the firm of Lowenstein and Newman to represent the utility at the hearings, and he was joined by Dow attorney Milton Wessel. Both lawyers filed frequent complaints with the Commission regarding the prolongation of the licensing process, but they too were ineffective in shortening the duration of the hearings. The Commission did not issue a construction permit for the Midland plant until December 15, 1972, two years after the start of the public hearings.

The Effect of the Administrative Process

Just as the Commission is criticized by both the environmental groups and the nuclear industry nationally, so it succeeded in pleasing neither at Midland. It was trying to guarantee that its licensing procedures complied with statutory requirements so that the hearings process and construction permit would not be invalidated on appeal to the courts.

Nevertheless, the intervenors charged the Commission with bias in support of the nuclear industry. In the exception to the ASLB issuance of a construction permit that the Mapleton and Saginaw Intervenors filed with the Atomic Safety and Licensing Appeal Board on January 15, 1973, they specifically noted that an article in the *Columbia Law Review* written by ASLB Chairman Arthur Murphy[37] before the Midland hearings ever began showed that he "had already made up his mind about the Midland case"[38] before the start of the public hearings. The intervenors charged further that the ASLB had not adequately resolved a number of questions concerning the Midland plant's effect on public health and safety. However, the Atomic Safety and Licensing Appeal Board affirmed the initial ASLB ruling on May 18, 1973.

Although the Midland construction permit had eventually been issued, the utility was equally dissatisfied with the Commission's licensing process. Consumers Power Company was especially critical of the ASLB for accepting the intervenors' requests for delays and letting them file a multitude of interrogatories requiring responses and then engage in the lengthy cross-examination that eventually amounted to more than 9000 pages of testimony and two years of construction delay.

It should be noted, however, that there were important external factors beyond the control of the environmental groups that contributed to the duration of the licensing process. It was in the midst of the Midland hearings, on July 23, 1971, that the Court of Appeals handed down its ruling in the Calvert Cliffs case which forced the Commission to issue new regulations requiring an environmental impact statement for each nuclear plant. Consequently, Consumers Power was asked to submit, in October, 1971, a supplemental environmental report which the Commission reviewed to assess the Midland plant's compliance with the new regulation. Also, the Commission's emergency core cooling system (ECCS) rulemaking hearings began in January, 1972, and continued through the remaining months of the Midland hearings. At one point, the ASLB adjourned the hearings to attend a conference on the ECCS, and delays were also caused by the Commission's issuance of interim standards for the ECCS forcing the Midland plant to be redesigned for compliance.

During the construction permit hearings, it was necessary for Consumers Power to halt its construction activity and design engineering for the Midland plant. Construction was stopped from November, 1970, until June, 1973. The result was a huge escalation in the projected cost of the Midland plant which Consumers Power found difficult to absorb. The projected cost was $349 million when the plant was first begun. By the time the ASLB hearings began in December, 1970, the projected cost had risen to $485 million, and it was $765 million when the construction permit was issued in December, 1972. By late 1974 when the Court of Appeals heard the case, the projected cost was already about a billion dollars. The increases could be partially attributed to the intervenors' success in extending the regulatory hearings and impeding construction for the two-year period, thereby exacerbating the inflationary increases in the cost of labor and equipment. Cost increases were also attributable to changes in regulatory requirements and to alterations of the project scope and design.[39] Furthermore, because of the delay in the Midland plant's completion, Consumers Power was forced to build two other non-nuclear plants to supply its customers' electric needs, thereby putting additional financial strain on the utility.

The detrimental financial impact on Consumers Power may best be described by saying that there were rumors that the company was near bankruptcy in the mid-1970s, thanks both to the Midland plant costs and to other problems that were common to all utilities at that time (see chapter 1). Consumers Power's financial difficulties forced the utility to postpone the construction of the Midland plant for most of 1975, thereby setting back by two years the target date for the plant's completion. As a result of this second construction setback, the projected cost of the nuclear plant went up again, reaching $1.67 billion in 1976. Thus, the delays in the construction permit licensing hearings had badly undermined the financial stability of the utility before the beginning of the years of litigation.

Summary and Conclusions

It is now possible to make a general comparison of the interest groups in the Midland nuclear plant dispute prior to the beginning of litigation: the anti-nuclear Saginaw and Mapleton Intervenors on the one hand and, on the other hand, the nuclear industry represented by Consumers Power Company with Dow Chemical Company's support. Each group had consistent ideological motivations, as well as a cohesive organizational framework. However, the environmental groups conformed to the popular stereotype of public interest groups in that they were held together primarily by the personal commitment and leadership of one person: Mary Sinclair. It was she who developed coalitions with other organizations and raised funds to retain Myron Cherry as the attorney for the intervenors in the construction permit hearings. The effectiveness of her group's ad hoc organization and minimal funding were maximized by Cherry's tactics. His strategy consisted of prolonging the hearings process so that it could be used as a means of public education and concurrently increase the cost of building the nuclear power plant.

The nuclear industry at Midland, as part of the business establishment, initially appeared to have more extensive resources than those of the environmental groups. Consumers Power Company not only benefited from its own corporate resources but also those of Dow Chemical Company. Furthermore, the utility had a broad coalition of societal support reinforcing its leadership and funding. The local supporters of the nuclear plant generated public pressure to expedite the hearings process, and the utility attorneys made frequent requests to the Atomic Safety and Licensing Board that the licensing be hastened.

However, partly because of the intervenor's use of dilatory tactics and partly because of events not directly related to the Midland plant, the construction permit hearings lasted for two years. Although the permit was eventually issued, delay greatly increased the projected expense of the plant and exacerbated Consumers Power's other financial constraints, ultimately causing an additional postponement in the plant's construction and a further escalation in its costs.

After the regulatory process was exhausted, the Midland construction permit could be appealed for judicial review. Thus, the litigation concerned the favorable Commission ruling on the plant's construction, and the litigants were two well-organized and effectively mobilized interest groups, with the nuclear industry already diminished in its capability by the duration and costliness of the licensing process. The licensing, however, was just a prelude to the lengthy litigation that would follow.

6

The Midland Case in the U.S. Court of Appeals

This chapter examines the judicial review of the Commission's Midland ruling in the United States Court of Appeals for the District of Columbia Circuit. Legal advocacy, meaning here the request for judicial review of the Midland plant construction permit, represented another tactic in the environmental groups' efforts to halt the plant's construction. However, legal advocacy as an interest group strategy usually involves not only filing a suit but also working to achieve a favorable judicial ruling. Interest groups may affect judicial policymaking through the choice of court in which a suit is filed, through the solicitation of friend-of-the-court briefs, through the generation of sympathetic law review articles and other legal scholarship, through the promotion of favorable media coverage, and through the encouragement of supportive public opinion. Therefore, the extent of the interest group efforts to influence the nature of the judicial ruling on Midland will be examined.

Finally, this chapter will also describe the impact of the court ruling on the litigants, as well as the impact of the litigation process itself in the aftermath of the court decision.

The Environmentalists' Decision to Use Legal Advocacy

As is directed by the Atomic Energy Act of 1954 and the Administrative Procedure Act of 1946, the issuance of a construction permit by the Commission may be appealed after all possible administrative remedies have been exhausted, as they had been at Midland. Chapters 3 and 4 explained that the environmentalists' favorable predisposition toward the use of litigation, combined with the detrimental effect it has previously had on the nuclear industry because of its duration, have resulted in frequent legal advocacy by antinuclear organizations. It is not surprising, therefore, that the Midland intervenors decided to appeal the nuclear plant construction permit to the courts. The intervenors' petitions to the United States Court of Appeals were made in July and August of 1973.

The environmentalists' attorney Myron Cherry warned Mary Sinclair and the other intervenors that they had little chance of winning a favorable judicial ruling regarding the Midland plant since the courts had usually deferred to the Commission and confirmed its decisions.[1] However, there were compensating advantages to litigation, as there had been to intervention in the public licensing hearings, that overrode any unfavorable rulings: the intervenors believed that the litigation process would focus public attention on the dangers of nuclear power that the Commission had overlooked in granting the construction permit for the plant.[2]

In addition to educating the public, the intervenors used litigation as another means of delaying the conclusion of the licensing process. As long as the validity of the construction permit remained tied up in the courts, there was no certainty that the plant would ever get final authorization. By further prolonging the licensing process, Cherry was trying to make building the nuclear plant "as painful and expensive as possible for the utility" so that its commitment to nuclear power would waver.[3]

Prior to the filing of the Midland plant suit in the federal court, the environmental groups had already tried legal advocacy in the Michigan state court system. The Mapleton Intervenors had brought suit against Consumers Power Company in 1973 claiming that the plant constituted a private and public nuisance and seeking money damages of $750,000. In this case known as *Marshall* v. *Consumers Power Company,* the Michigan Court of Appeals ruled against the intervenors. The court decided that the existence of the nuclear plant did not, by itself, constitute a nuisance, and the state was preempted from consideration of atomic energy safety questions.[4] Thus, the suit which the intervenors filed in the U.S. Court of Appeals represented the second judicial involvement with the Midland plant.

Some observers believe that Consumers Power Company would have been wise to file a countersuit in the U.S. Court of Appeals against Cherry and the boards of directors of the intervenor groups at the conclusion of the Commission's construction permit hearings. They cite Cherry's skillful extension of the Midland public hearings as an "abuse of process" that would constitute grounds for such a suit.[5]

However, Consumers Power did not decide to use legal advocacy against the environmentalists. The utility had initially been granted the construction permit it had sought and saw no reason to appeal a favorable ruling. In addition, delay of the hearings, which had been the major problem, is difficult to subject to litigation and litigation could only extend the adjudicatory process even further. In any case, Consumers Power believed that the duration and thoroughness of the public hearings had added to the validity of the Midland plant's permit. The Court of Appeals was expected to further confirm the Commission's ruling. Furthermore, the utility was constantly on the defensive, and its attorney explained that the legal staff was "too busy putting out fires to start any" by instigating a new lawsuit.[6]

The Ruling on the Midland Nuclear Plant

On November 27, 1974, approximately two years after the Commission initially granted a construction permit for the Midland nuclear plant, the Court of Appeals for the District of Columbia Circuit heard the arguments appealing the issuance of the permit. The cases were entitled *Nelson Aeschliman et al. v. United States Nuclear Regulatory Commission* and *Saginaw Valley Nuclear Study Group et al. v. United States Nuclear Regulatory Commission.*[7] The former case was brought by the group referred to as the Mapleton Intervenors, and the latter case represented the appeal of the six groups that had formed a coalition to intervene in the licensing hearings under the leadership of the Saginaw Valley Nuclear Study Group (the Sierra Club, West Michigan Environmental Action Council, the United Auto Workers, Citizens Committee for Environmental Protection of Michigan, and the University of Michigan Environmental Law Society). An additional brief in support of the petitioners was filed by the State of Kansas, a party with belated involvement in the licensing intervention. Thus, there had been no change in the composition of the antinuclear environmental groups opposing the Midland plant between the administrative hearings process and the Court of Appeals cases.

As indicated in the case names, the Commission was the primary respondent or defendant in the litigation. Consumers Power Company, whose construction permit for the Midland plant was at stake, filed a lengthy brief in support of the Commission's position. Dow Chemical Company did not file a brief in the case.

The Court of Appeals handed down its ruling on the Midland case on July 21, 1976, and ruled at the same time on *Natural Resources Defense Council v. United States Nuclear Regulatory Commission.*[8] As in most litigation involving nuclear plant licensing, the issues presented for judicial review in the Midland case were substantially the same as many of those raised by the intervenors during the Commission's public licensing hearings. Although the court dismissed some of the issues that the intervenors had raised,[9] the judicial ruling was sympathetic to four of the environmentalists' concerns. The court remanded the Midland construction permit to the Commission for clarification of the Advisory Committee on Reactor Safeguards (ACRS) report, reconsideration of the impact of energy conservation, reevaluation of the Dow Chemical Company's need for the plant, and consideration of the nuclear waste disposal issue.[10] Two of these matters, conservation considerations and the resolution of the waste management problem, had far-reaching significance for the nuclear industry as a whole.

Prior to the start of the Atomic Safety and Licensing Board (ASLB) public hearings for a construction permit, Consumers Power's application to build a reactor had been examined over a twenty-two month period by the staff of the Commission and, independently, by the ACRS. The ACRS is a body of up to fifteen scientifically-trained, part-time consultants that makes an evaluation of each reactor license application independently of and in addition to the Commission staff's review. It was created by Congress in 1957 as a watchdog committee that would make a public report on the safety of each reactor prior to public hearings and administrative decision making on the issuance of reactor licenses.

After reviewing the Midland plant construction permit application, the ACRS issued two reports, the first on June 18, 1970, concluding that the plant would not endanger public health and safety. However, it was the language used in this five-page report that stimulated questions from the Saginaw Intervenors. The ACRS report stated in part:

> Other problems related to large water reactors have been identified by the Regulatory Staff and the ACRS and cited in previous ACRS reports. The Committee believes that resolution of these items should apply equally to the Midland Plant Units 1 and 2. The Committee (ACRS) believes that the above items can be resolved during construction and that, if due consideration is given to these items, the nuclear units proposed for the Midland Plant can be constructed with reasonable assurance that they can be operated without undue risk to the health and safety of the public.[11]

The Saginaw Intervenors then "sought discovery from the ACRS concerning what those 'problems' and 'items' were, what 'due consideration' the ACRS thought they should be given, and why the ACRS 'believes' that the problems 'could be resolved during construction'."[12] Although the intervenors' discovery requests were granted for massive amounts of Commission and utility documents and answers to hundreds of interrogatories, the ASLB denied their discovery requests to members of the ACRS panel. The Commission based this refusal on its contention that the ACRS report is "a collegial document reflecting the collective view of the Committee as a whole"[13] so that no one member or group of members can speak for the whole panel. The Court of Appeals agreed with the Commission, ruling "against the propriety of discovery directed to individual ACRS members and ACRS documents."[14]

However, the court remanded the ACRS report to the ACRS for "clarification of ambiguities," saying that it "should have provided a short explanation, understandable to a layman, of the additional matters of concern to the committee."[15] The court based its ruling on legislative intent, citing the role that Congress had intended for the ACRS to fill in 1957 when its establishment became part of the Atomic Energy Act. The court quoted from a statement from the Congressional Joint Committee on Atomic Energy: "The report of the ACRS committee is to be made public so that all concerned may be apprised of the safety or possible hazards of the facility."[16]

The second issue on which the court remanded the Midland construction permit to the Commission for further consideration involved the question of energy conservation. The Saginaw Intervenors had argued that the environmental impact statement (EIS) for the Midland plant did not adequately conform to the National Environmental Policy Act (NEPA). Sections 102 (C) (iii) and 102 (D) of NEPA require that the EIS consider "alternatives to the proposed action," and the intervenors asserted that one alternative not adequately examined by the Commission was the lack of need for the plant if a reduction of demand for electricity through energy conservation was encouraged.[17]

When the matter of conservation had come before the ASLB initially, it had cited the "rule of reason"[18] in its refusal "to inquire into whether the customary uses being made of electricity in our society are 'proper' or 'improper'." The ASLB said that the "'real question' was which power generating technology would be superior."[19] Later the ASLAB had affirmed this position, holding that the cost–benefit analysis undertaken by the Commission had inherently dealt with the alternative of not constructing the plant at all. Consumers Power Company detailed the forecast regarding future demand for electricity in Michigan from the Federal Power Commission, the Michigan Public Service Commission, and the Environmental Protection Agency that originally went into the Draft Environmental Statement for the Commission.

However, the intervenors contended that the Commission should have investigated not only the expected electricity forecast for Michigan but also the ways in which customary electricity usage could be cut back through customer behavior modifications, such as a different rate structure or changes in utility advertising. As the intervenors pointed out, an ASLB in a subsequent 1973 licensing proceeding for another plant decided that these means to potential electricity conservation were worthy of consideration. By way of justification for not having explored the conservation matter more fully in the Midland hearings, the Commission claimed that the Saginaw Intervenors had not, during the licensing process, made an adequate case by using supporting data or even defining the meaning of conservation. The Commission's brief contends, "Saginaw had only itself to blame for failing to make a case here. Despite its own failures, Saginaw seeks to shift to the Commission the entire responsibility for examining all issues concerning energy conservation."[20] In other words, the Commission was applying a "threshold test," meaning that the intervenors had to take responsibility for stating clearly the specifics of an argument (energy conservation, in this case) before the Commission would study it seriously.

The court opinion strongly objected to the Commission's placement of the burden of proof on the intervenors. The court repeated its interpretation of NEPA, earlier elucidated in the case of *Calvert Cliffs Coordinating Committee* v. *AEC,* that it is the responsibility only of the Commission to take the initiative in assembling data regarding conservation as an alternative and not merely "sit back, like an umpire, and resolve adversary contentions at the hearing stage."[21] Again referring to the Calvert Cliffs opinion, the court repeated that "it is unrealistic to assume that there will always be an intervenor with the information, energy, and money required" to adequately air environmental issues.[22] Stating that the Commission's rejection of the need to study the energy conservation issue on the basis of the "threshold test" was "capricious and arbitrary," the court remanded the issue to the Commission so that it could reach its own "rational judgment."[23]

In ruling that the Commission should undertake its own investigation of the true need for the electricity which the Midland plant would generate, the court also cautioned the Commission to "take into account the changed circumstances regarding Dow's need for process steam, and the intended continued operation of Dow's fossil-fueled generating facilities."[24] The court was here referring to the renegotiated contract between Consumers Power and Dow which had been announced in February, 1974. Although the original contract had specified that the Midland plant would replace Dow's obsolete coal-fired plant, the Saginaw Intervenors pointed out that the new contract allowed Dow to maintain its old plant. Consumers Power countered, however, that the fossil-fueled plant would be maintained only on a standby basis and that there had been no change in the Dow commitment to purchase large amounts of process steam, as well as electricity. The court's ruling, in effect, told the Commission to be careful to monitor any further changes in the Dow–Consumers contractual agreements.[25]

The court decision in the Midland case with regard to the fuel cycle or radioactive waste management issue was controlled by its opinions, handed down on the same day, in *Natural Resources Defense Council* v. *United States Nuclear Regulatory Commission.*[26] This case had been argued before the Court of Appeals six months after the Midland case, on May 27, 1975. It involved the operating license authorized by the Commission for the Vermont Yankee nuclear plant in Vernon, Vermont, as well as the validity of the Commission's generic rulemaking in 1974 regarding nuclear waste management. It was the decision of the Court of Appeals that the two cases' rulings be issued simultaneously, and both the Midland environmentalists and Consumers Power Company were sorry to see them combined.[27]

In the Midland case, the Saginaw Intervenors charged that the "AEC's refusal to consider the environmental and economic consequences of radioactive waste production by the Midland plant violates both the National

Environmental Policy Act and the principles of due process.''[28] The Natural Resources Defense Council (NRDC) had made similar charges in regard to the Commission's issuance of an operating license for the Vermont Yankee plant, which had then been in operation since 1972.

The parties involved in appealing the Vermont Yankee case included not only the NRDC, the environmental litigation group, but also the New England Coalition on Nuclear Pollution which was a local antinuclear group contesting the Vermont Yankee plant, and the Consolidated National Intervenors, a coalition of eighty public interest groups including the Sierra Club and the Union of Concerned Scientists. It should be noted that the congruence of aims of the Saginaw Intervenors and the environmental groups involved in the NRDC case was a natural result of Myron Cherry's representation of the Consolidated National Intervenors in the ECCS hearings and Mary Sinclair's position as a codirector of that group.

On the other side, the NRDC case included, as respondents, the Nuclear Regulatory Commission with the Vermont Yankee Nuclear Power Corporation, the utility directly involved, plus the Baltimore Gas and Electric Company and fourteen other utilities that were part of the original rulemaking proceedings. Several additional utilities formed a coalition to submit another friend-of-the-court brief in support of the nuclear industry. Just as the State of Kansas had submitted a brief urging reversal of the construction permit in the Midland case, so the State of New York urged reversal in the Vermont Yankee case.

Specifically, the Vermont Yankee case involved the adequacy of the 1974 Commission's generic rulemaking regarding the environmental impact of radioactive waste management. At that proceeding, the only expert information regarding waste management was given by Dr. Frank Pittman, Director of the Commission's Division of Waste Management and Transportation. Chief Judge Bazelon, who wrote the opinion in the Vermont Yankee case, as he had in the Midland case noted that Pittman's testimony was lacking in citations, references or other documentation and consisted of ''extremely vague assurances by agency personnel that problems as yet unsolved will be solved.''[29]

On the basis of Pittman's testimony, the Commission had then gone on to promulgate a rule expressing in numerical terms the incremental contribution of each individual reactor's waste to the environmental impact of the waste management problem. The Commission concluded from the rule that the waste from each plant would be too small to have any real significance.

Judge Bazelon held that the rulemaking, which was a legislative administrative procedure, had not been sufficiently thorough in identifying pertinent evidence nor in articulating careful reasoning. His concern was that both sides of the waste disposal question had not been given proper consideration and ventilation by the Commission. Consequently, the court ruled that the Commission had violated the provision of the National Environmental Policy Act (NEPA) mandating an informed decision–making process and had exercised "capricious and arbitrary" judgment in violation of the Administrative Procedure Act.[30]

In this opinion, then, the court was directly involved in the substantive issues of the Commission's rule regarding nuclear waste disposal. By way of explanation, Bazelon wrote:

> Of necessity, assessing agency procedures requires that the reviewing court immerse itself in the record. Abstract characterizations are an unsatisfactory guide for determining what procedures are necessary in particular proceedings . . . . This does not give the court a license to judge for itself how much weight should be given particular pieces of scientific or technical data, a task for which it is singularly ill–suited. It does require, however, that the court examine the record so that it may satisfy itself that the decision was based 'on a consideration of the relevant factors.'[31]

Thus, the court concluded that NEPA mandated judicial oversight of administrative procedures concerning environmental protection.

The court ordered the Commission's original rule regarding nuclear waste management to be remanded for renewed consideration. Judge Bazelon, in a separate statement, suggested the use of a hybrid procedure, involving informal rulemaking but with a mixture of adjudicatory and legislative procedures that would permit more input from the environmental groups whose views differed from Dr. Pittman's.[32]

Judge Edward A. Tamm, who served as the third member of the three-judge panel for the Vermont Yankee case, along with David Bazelon and George C. Edwards, wrote a concurring opinion in which he differed with Judge Bazelon's preference for hybrid rulemaking. He expressed concern that the court's suggestion of additional procedures would result in "over-formalization" of agency procedures. Judge Tamm preferred simply to remand the Commission's rule for more documentation.[33] Thus, the Court of Appeals was refraining from making obligatory procedural prescriptions while insisting that the issue of waste management be more thoroughly explored by the Commission.

Because the court held that the Commission's generic rulemaking had proven ineffective, the judges concluded that the individual licensing proceedings of both the Midland and Vermont Yankee plants would have to be reopened. In the absence of a generic rule on the effects of nuclear waste disposal, the licensing boards of the two plants in question would have to deal with the problem themselves.[34] Thus, the Midland plant's construction permit was remanded to the Commission for reconsideration.

Influences on the Court of Appeals Ruling

A judicial ruling favorable to an interest group may be the result, in part, of the group's strategy in influencing the course of the litigation.[35] There are a number of tactics which a group may employ in working to achieve a favorable judicial opinion. As explained in chapter 4, one of the most significant of these tactics is the choice of the court in which a case is to be heard. The aggrieved party in a regulatory ruling, that is, the party that first files suit, has the prerogative of selecting the court. The suit against the Midland plant could have been filed either in the Sixth Circuit Court of Appeals that services Michigan or in the Court of Appeals for the District of Columbia Circuit. The Midland environmentalists were the aggrieved party that appealed the Commission's issuance of a construction permit, and it was their choice to have the D.C. Circuit hear the case.

The Court of Appeals for the District of Columbia Circuit was the obvious choice for the Midland suit since it was generally regarded as a liberal court and had frequently ruled in favor of environmental and consumer groups. The court then had the record of often remanding cases to adminstrative agencies for procedural improvements. In fact, the D.C. Circuit had so often ruled against the federal agencies that many Justice Department lawyers were especially wary of that particular Court of Appeals.[36] There were three conservative, Nixon-appointed judges on the nine-member court in 1976 (McKinnon, Wilkey, and Robb); and the three-judge panels that were composed to rule on appellate cases usually included just one of these judges, plus two others with more liberal inclinations.[37]

The D.C. Circuit's record on nuclear-related cases was consistent with its other rulings. Its best-known decision had been *Calvert Cliffs Coordinating Committee* v. *AED,*[38] the opinion which had had the most far-reaching and detrimental effect on the development of nuclear power. The Calvert Cliffs opinion was written by Judge Skelly Wright with Judges Tamm and Robinson comprising the remainder of the panel. Judge Wright's language in the case made clear his criticism of the nuclear plant licensing process and his sharp rebuke of the Commission for its failure to comply with the provisions of NEPA.

Some of the other nuclear cases that came before the D.C. Circuit had also served to restructure the Commission's licensing process. In 1975, the year prior to the Midland decision, the D.C. Circuit had instructed the Commission to clearly articulate and explain its decision-making processes (*Nader* v. *NRC*),[39] to particularize the radiation emission standards for each nuclear plant (*York Committee for a Safe Environment* v. *NRC*),[40] to utilize risk-benefit analysis prior to licensing each plant (*Citizens for Safe Power, Inc.* v. *NRC*),[41] and to consider alternatives to nuclear power such as energy conservation (*Carolina Environmental Study Group* v. *United States*).[42] Thus, the D.C. Court had shown itself to be willing to exercise judicial review of nuclear power decision making and to independently reassess Commission rulings.

Judge David Bazelon, the Chief Judge of the Court of Appeals for the District of Columbia Circuit, heard the Midland case along with Judge Charles Fahy and Judge William Wayne Justice, a U.S. District Court Judge for the Eastern District of Texas. It was Chief Judge Bazelon who wrote the Midland opinion. He was already well known for his administrative law rulings, having previously exercised significant influence in the expansion of judicial review of agency actions. Accordingly, Judge Bazelon had helped to institute changes in the standing doctrine; he had urged agencies to independently investigate issues beyond those that the parties had presented; he had insisted on careful agency explanations of the reasons behind their decisions; and he had urged the promulgation by agencies of general policies and comprehensive regulatory guidelines.[43]

Judge Bazelon had previously expressed particular concern for judicial review of administrative decisions involving scientific matters. In *Environmental Defense Fund* v. *Ruckelshaus,* he had said that issues involving "fundamental personal interests in life, health and property" should have a "special claim to judicial protection."[44] He thought that technical questions should be thoroughly explored by administrative agencies and "resolved in the crucible of debate through the clash of informed but opposing scientific and technological viewpoints" before they come before the courts (*International Harvester Co.* v. *Ruckelshaus*)[45] Bazelon's eagerness to have agencies thoroughly examine both sides of scientific questions was based on his own concern that he and other judges are "technically illiterate" and unqualified, therefore, to make informed choices among advisable scientific alternatives (*Ethyl Corp.* v. *EPA*).[46] Bazelon believed that many of these ostensibly scientific decisions actually involved "basic philosophic issues," as in the nuclear waste management case.[47] Thus, the Midland ruling was completely consistent with the previous opinions handed down by the D.C. Circuit and by Chief Judge David Bazelon in particular. The Saginaw and Mapleton Intervenors' choice of that court as the best one in which to file their appeal was clearly vindicated.

A second potential interest group tactic to influence judicial decision making is the solicitation of supportive friend-of-the-court briefs to bolster the parties' own briefs. Before the judiciary, support for the parties to a case must come not from letters and telegrams to the judges or from picket signs outside the courthouse but, rather, from these friend-of-the-court briefs (amicus curiae briefs). Friend-of-the-court briefs help demonstrate the numbers of people supporting the parties' positions and serve notice to the court that there are others less directly involved in the particular case who also favor a certain judicial outcome. The briefs themselves are often useful in arguing points of law that were not mentioned in the parties' briefs. The friends-of-the-court may raise legal arguments that are more general or less reliant on precedent than the narrow legal grounds on which a defendant often rests his case.

Friend-of-the-court briefs are usually more numerous in Supreme Court Cases than in lower court litigation. In the Midland and Vermont Yankee cases before the Court of Appeals, Consumers Power intervened in support of the Commission, as did a utility coalition. The states of Kansas and New York, however, contributed friends' briefs for the environmentalists. The nuclear industry may have been weakened by the absence of a Dow Chemical Company brief on behalf of Consumers Power Company and the Commission. Although Dow had initially been granted permission to intervene and had helped promote the development of the Midland plant during the construction permit hearings, Dow had filed a motion with the Court of Appeals for leave to withdraw on March 7, 1974, before the case was heard. Perhaps, therefore, the court interpreted the withdrawal as a decrease in Dow's need for the plant. In any case, the court ruling specifically instructed the Commission to monitor future Dow-Consumers Power contractual agreements.

A third potential interest group influence on judicial decision making is current legal scholarship: the commentary on judicial opinions and practices found in law reviews and other legal journals. It is widely understood that these writings have a definite effect not only on the lawyers but also on judges, especially evidenced by the fact that law review articles are frequently cited in court opinions. Sometimes the authors of legal articles are students or professors making a general summary of judicial precedents regarding some point of law, but more frequently the authors are advocating a specific legal position and providing supporting arguments for it. These advocates thereby further the cause of some parties to cases and hurt the chances of others. In fact, it has been charged in Congress that law review articles may have excessive impact on judicial decision making.[48]

Since the publication of favorable legal scholarship often has a positive effect on judicial opinions, it is sometimes the members of the interest groups involved in litigation who write articles for the legal periodicals about the matter under adjudication. In regard to the Midland and Vermont Yankee cases, Anthony Roisman, an NRDC lawyer in the latter case, published an article in *Trial* in January-February, 1974, the year that the Court of Appeals heard arguments on Midland. His topic in the article "Suing for Safety" was the proindustry bias of the Commission and the fact that environmental groups often resorted to litigation appealing the

Commission's rulings in order to let both sides of the nuclear controversy be aired.[49] Although Chief Judge Bazelon did not cite this article in his opinion, it is possible that he did read it.

Just as Judge Bazelon expects administrative decisions to be well documented, so he is also careful to explain his own decision-making process with appropriate citations and footnotes. Consequently, it is possible to determine which articles have particularly impressed him and influenced his ruling. The body of legal literature from which he drew his documentation in these cases included a lively debate regarding administrative rulemaking procedure that had been taking place on the pages of the law reviews in the two years prior to the issuance of the Midland opinion. The seven articles cited by Bazelon discussed agency informal rulemaking, as well as judicial review of those rules, and the debate particularly concerned the administrative procedures best-suited to guarantee the formulation of a well-reasoned rule.[50] Bazelon, of course, selected the hybrid approach recommended by Williams as the most useful one.[51] In so doing, Bazelon was not responding directly to either the pro- or antinuclear legal scholarship, but rather to the advocates of a more thorough and equitable administrative decision making.

A fourth potential interest group influence on judicial decisionmaking is the promotion of favorable media coverage. The Court of Appeals rulings on Midland and Vermont Yankee especially reflected a grasp of the concerns about nuclear power expressed by antinuclear environmentalists in the media at the time the opinion was written. Bazelon was clearly troubled by the degree of toxicity of radioactive wastes and the length of time that they would remain hazardous to the public. He quoted in a footnote from a 1974 article by D. Farney in the *Smithsonian Magazine* entitled "Ominous Problem: What to Do with Radioactive Waste" and saying, "The entire recorded history of mankind is but a fraction of the 250,000 year storage time of plutonium."[52]

Similarly, Bazelon's perusal of the media had convinced him that the government lacked the commitment to a specific waste disposal methodology; and he cited "ERDA Shelves a Nuclear Waste Storage Plan" in *Science* magazine of April 25, 1975, to document that belief.[53] Bazelon's awareness of the complications with the government's earlier plan to bury wastes in salt beds is documented by his citation of Boffey, "Radioactive Waste Site Search Gets into Deep Water", in *Science* of October 24, 1975,[54] and "Salt, Rock Formations Favored for A-Wastes" in the *Washington Post* on May 11, 1976.[55] Finally, he also expressed concern regarding low-level radioactive wastes, mentioning "New Alarms About Old Nuclear Wastes" in *Business Week* of February 2, 1976,[56] and "GAO Reports New Nuclear Garbage Problem" in *Science and Government Report* of February 1, 1976.[57] Thus, the Court of Appeals ruling itself testifies to the impression made on the judges by the media coverage given to the potential hazards of nuclear wastes.

It should be noted, however, that Chief Judge Bazelon's citations of the current literature on nuclear power were very selective. Bazelon was a periodic participant in the meetings on a variety of topics held by the American Assembly, a nonpartisan forum sponsored by Columbia University, which brought together more than sixty scholars and industrial and governmental leaders to discuss the future of nuclear energy in April, 1976. Although Bazelon did not attend that symposium, he received the summary of its report that spring since he was on their mailing list. Consequently, he selectively extracted a quotation from the report in his Midland ruling, saying that "scholars and government officials are almost unanimous that energy conservation will have an important, although not decisive, role in overall energy policy in coming decades."[58] Actually, the major conclusion of the American Assembly had been its assertion that the development of nuclear energy was essential. The symposium had also agreed that potential risks arising from the storage of radioactive wastes could be handled with the scientific expertise then available,[59] but Chief Judge Bazelon's opinion on Midland mentioned neither of these other findings.

A fifth potential interest group influence on judicial decision making is the encouragement of supportive public opinion. Although most judicial rulings do not follow the election returns, as is sometimes charged, judges' attitudes are often affected by the public's perception of a case. As described in chapter 5, local public opinion in the town of Midland favored the development of a nuclear plant there. However, public opinion on nuclear power in general[60] and the specific endorsement of the nuclear plant by the Midland community were not used to try to influence the Court of Appeals decision. The judges were probably not even aware of the extent of local enthusiasm for the plant. The only brief mentioning public endorsement at all was that of the Commission which made only a vague, one-sentence reference to the community's position in a footnote, thereby losing the opportunity to try to inform the court about favorable public opinion. Judge Bazelon's concern about the public is evident from a statement in his opinion: "The public—the 'guinea pigs' who will bear the consequences of either resolution of the nuclear controversy—is apprehensive."[61] Bazelon was certainly correct about the antinuclear environmental groups being "apprehensive," but he was wrong about public opinion in the Midland community as a whole.

It may be concluded that both sets of interest groups in the Midland case did little to actively influence the outcome of the judicial policymaking process in the Court of Appeals in the way that interest groups have traditionally been able to exercise influence. The only major input into the use of legal advocacy that became a determinant of the nature of the court's ruling was the environmentalists' choice of the sympathetic Court of Appeals for the D.C. Circuit as the best court in which to file suit. The fact that it was Chief Judge Bazelon who heard the Midland and Vermont Yankee cases clearly affected the judicial output.

Aftermath of the Court Ruling

The Court of Appeals rulings in the Midland and Vermont Yankee cases regarding both the nuclear fuel cycle and the conservation question had a far-reaching effect on the Commission's licensing procedures. On August 13, 1976, the Commission made a policy statement announcing temporary suspension of nuclear plant licensing, just as it had done after the Calvert Cliffs opinion. The Commission decided to defer the issuance of construction permits or operating licenses that were then pending for eleven other nuclear plants.

In the meantime, the Commission announced that it would hold a new rulemaking proceeding on the nuclear waste issue. To prepare for this proceeding, the Commission began an extensive analysis of the environmental impact of fuel reprocessing and waste management, trying to put together a more thorough and well-documented determination of their cost for each individual nuclear plant. The revised survey was completed about three months after the Court of Appeals decision had been handed down. Its findings differed little from the Commission's original rule regarding cost-benefit analysis for each plant and again concluded that the environmental impact of the management of the nuclear waste from each individual reactor would be insignificant. On the basis of this finding, the Court of Appeals told the Commission to resume the licensing of nuclear plants in early November, 1976, pending the formal rulemaking proceedings. In the meantime, however, the Commission's licenses would be issued conditionally and would be dependent upon the successful resolution of the administrative and judicial procedures.

After the Court of Appeals handed down its ruling on Midland, intervenor attorney Myron Cherry wrote to the Commission saying that, on the basis of the court opinion, the Midland licensing hearings should be reopened to determine whether the construction permit ought to be revoked or modified. In August, 1976, at the same time that the Commission temporarily suspended all nuclear plant licensing, it also agreed to Cherry's request and began to reexamine the Midland construction permit, as well as the Vermont Yankee operating license. A new Atomic Safety and Licensing Board (ASLB) was subsequently assembled for each of the two plants, and the Midland construction permit suspension hearings began in Chicago in November, 1976. It was not until September of the following year that the

ASLB finally decided not to suspend construction of the Midland plant pending the conclusion of the ongoing regulatory hearings and the judicial review of the Midland construction permit.

Summary and Conclusions

The Midland environmental groups appealed the issuance of the nuclear plant's construction permit to the courts even though they did not expect to obtain a favorable judicial ruling. Rather, legal advocacy was the environmentalists' strategy to extend further the duration of the licensing process and to focus public attention on the dangers of nuclear power. Consumers Power Company agreed with the environmental groups that the Court of Appeals ruling would probably defer to the Commission's issuance of a permit for the Midland plant. The utility waited for a favorable ruling and did not itself decide to use legal advocacy as a tactic for discouraging the environmentalists or expediting the regulatory process.

With the nuclear plant's construction permit subject to judicial review, the Commission and the utility did little outside the appellate process to actively promote a favorable ruling. For instance, although Consumers Power intervened in support of the Commission, it did not try to persuade Dow Chemical Company which needed the plant's process steam to submit a supporting brief.[62] Furthermore, public opinion regarding the nuclear plant was hardly brought to the judge's attention.

The antinuclear groups did little more than the nuclear industry to influence the outcome of the judicial process. However, their choice of the U.S. Court of Appeals for the D.C. Circuit as the best court in which to file suit meant that the majority of the judges had a previous record of sympathy with environmental groups. Chief Judge David Bazelon who wrote the opinions in both the Midland and Vermont Yankee cases was especially predisposed toward judicial review of administrative decision making and thorough ventilation of technical issues. Thus, the environmental groups' selection of the D.C. Circuit did favorably influence the judicial policy-making process for them.

The impact of the judicial opinion was very detrimental to the nuclear industry and the Commission. The court ordered the Commission to begin a new rulemaking proceeding on the nuclear waste issue, and the nuclear industry as a whole was affected by the temporary suspension of nuclear plant licensing. In addition, the duration of the regulatory process for the Midland plant was further extended. The construction permit that Consumers Power Company had received for the Midland plant in 1972 was, in 1976, remanded to a new Atomic Safety and Licensing Board for reconsideration, as was the operating license of the Vermont Yankee nuclear plant which was also involved in the court ruling. Although the Midland plant construction was allowed to continue, the certainty of the plant's eventual completion was jeopardized. Thus, the environmentalists' use of legal advocacy in the Court of Appeals had further debilitated the nuclear industry.

7

The Midland Case in the Supreme Court

This chapter will explain the nuclear industry's decision to use legal advocacy itself and appeal the Court of Appeals ruling to the Supreme Court. The Court's ruling will then be examined. As in chapter 6, the potential interest group influences on the Supreme Court as it made its ruling will be elucidated in order to investigate the reasons for the opinion and the extent of interest group involvement in the judicial policymaking process.

The Utility's Decision to Appeal

The decision to appeal the Court of Appeals ruling to the Supreme Court was made by the utilities, not by the Nuclear Regulatory Commission. The Commission had had three courses of action open to it after its judicial reprimand from the Court of Appeals. First, it could refrain from appealing the ruling and simply comply with the court prescriptions in regard to generic rulemaking procedures, as, in fact, the agency immediately began to do. After the even more critical judicial review of the Commission's licensing process in the Calvert Cliffs case, the agency had chosen not to appeal the ruling.

Secondly, it could ask the Court of Appeals to engage in an *en banc* review of the case in which the whole nine–judge panel would vote on the opinion. However, there was a general belief that the ruling by the three-judge panel in the Midland and Vermont Yankee cases probably reflected the attitudes of the majority of judges on the D.C. Circuit Court. Finally, the Commission could choose to appeal its case to the Supreme Court.

The agency had good reason to want to appeal the case. The Court of Appeals opinion had been ambiguous regarding proper rulemaking procedures and regarding the validity of the two licenses in question, as well as other plants' licenses, while the rulemaking proceeded. The Commission felt it needed further judicial directives. In addition, the agency believed that the court had interfered in its internal decision-making processes.[1] A Supreme Court reversal of the Court of Appeals opinion could potentially vindicate the agency's original procedures.

However, it was the utilities, Consumers Power Company and Vermont Yankee Nuclear Power Corporation, rather than the Commission, which initially, and separately, decided to ask for the higher court's review in

October, 1976. The utilities' decisions were made independently of each other.[2] Their actions were prompted by what they considered to be the Commission's overreaction to the Court of Appeals ruling. They were concerned because new Atomic Safety and Licensing Boards (ASLB) had been convened to reconsider their licenses, and Consumers Power charged that reopening the administrative hearings was "not only unfair to such licensees, it is an invitation to administrative anarchy."[3]

The precedent of judicial revocation of existing nuclear plant licenses was a threat to all utilities with nuclear plants. Several environmental groups had filed motions with the Commission after the court's ruling asking that licenses for about fifteen nuclear plants, in addition to the two in question, be suspended pending resolution of the waste disposal problem. Accordingly, the Seabrook, New Hampshire, nuclear plant's construction permit was initially suspended for reconsideration by the ASLB in October, 1976, and other plants' licenses were reviewed. Thus, the Court of Appeals decision could potentially shut down many nuclear plants.

There was no certainty that the Supreme Court would grant the writ of *certiorari* from the utilities. Having been generally satisfied with the Court of Appeals ruling, the Saginaw Intervenors submitted a petition in December, 1976, in opposition to the writ. However, the utilities' petition for certiorari had a better chance of acceptance when the Commission decided in January, 1977, to join in the utilities' request. The Commission's memorandum to the Supreme Court stated that the Court of Appeals opinion had interfered with the agency's authority and involved erroneous procedural rulings. Interestingly, however, the Commission's petition for a writ was coupled with a memorandum from the Justice Department which suggested that the Supreme Court deny the writ of certiorari on the grounds that the Midland and Vermont Yankee cases were not significant enough to warrant the Court's attention.[4] Nonetheless, the Supreme Court agreed to review the case in February, 1977, and the oral arguments were heard on November 28, 1977.

The Supreme Court Ruling on the Midland Plant

When the utilities acted independently of the Commission and appealed their cases to the Supreme Court, they became the petitioners and the environmental groups took the role of respondents. Since the Midland case was coupled with the Vermont Yankee case by the Supreme Court, the case names that appeared on the docket were *Vermont Yankee Nuclear Power Corp.* v. *Natural Resources Defense Council, Inc., et al. and Consumers Power Company* v. *Aeschliman, et al.*[5] The parties to the cases were, on the one hand, the two utilities, Consumers Power Company and Vermont

Yankee Nuclear Power Corporation, with the support of the Nuclear Regulatory Commission; and, on the other hand, the Saginaw and Mapleton Intervenors in the Midland case, and in the Vermont Yankee case, the Natural Resources Defense Council (NRDC), the Consolidated National Intervenors, and the New England Coalition on Nuclear Pollution. The Vermont Yankee Case involved only the radioactive waste disposal issue while the Midland case concerned not only that question but also the conservation issue and the ACRS report.

Justice William Rehnquist delivered the opinion of the Court on April 3, 1978. The others who took part in the 7 to 0 unanimous decision were Chief Justice Warren Burger and Justices William Brennan, Potter Stewart, Byron White, Thurgood Marshall, and John Paul Stevens. Justices Harry Blackmun and Lewis Powell were not involved in the Court's decision.

The opinion from the conservative Justice Rehnquist was strongly worded and decisively favored the nuclear industry's position. It sharply rebuked the Court of Appeals, and as *The New York Times* pointed out, "The Supreme Court was about as angry as it ever gets."[6] It accused the lower court of excessive judicial activism, of "judicial intervention run riot."[7]

The Court of Appeals ruling on the radioactive waste disposal issue was the first question to be reviewed in the Supreme Court opinion. The Midland intervenors had suggested that the waste question had only "tangential significance"[8] and was largely irrelevant to the issue of the Midland plant's construction permit. The NRDC had similarly advised that the waste disposal issue was already moot because of the Commission's new interim rule on waste disposal and its grant to the Vermont Yankee plant of an eighteen-month interim license. However, the utilities and the Commission had requested that the Supreme Court review the waste disposal question. They had suggested that the initial waste disposal rule be remanded to the Commission for better documentation but that the Court of Appeals' ideas about hybrid rulemaking procedures be dismissed.

The Rehnquist opinion followed the nuclear industry's recommendations on the waste disposal rule. Rehnquist considered the matter sufficiently important to merit Supreme Court review. He noted his awareness that the Vermont Yankee nuclear plant would produce "well over one hundred pounds of radioactive wastes, some of which will be highly toxic" and, therefore, "must be isolated for anywhere from six hundred to hundreds of thousands of years."[9] The Supreme Court concluded, as had the Court of Appeals, that the wastes have a sufficiently significant environmental impact to necessitate administrative agency examination under the provisions of the National Environmental Policy Act (NEPA).

The Supreme Court emphatically differed with the Court of Appeals, however, in regard to the Commission's rulemaking procedures. Rehnquist criticized with sarcasm the ambiguity of the Bazelon opinion: "But before determining whether the Court of Appeals reached a permissible result, we must determine exactly what result it did reach, and in this case that is no mean feat."[10] He concluded that the lower court appeared to have remanded the waste disposal rule to the Commission because of the "perceived inadequacies of the procedures employed in the rulemaking proceedings."[11] Both courts agreed that the Commission rulemaking procedures complied with Section 553 of the Administrative Procedure Act (APA) of 1946. Nonetheless, the Court of Appeals had ruled that NEPA allowed the judiciary to force agencies to go beyond the APA's minimal procedural requirements for rulemaking. However, Rehnquist cited judicial precedents[12] to demonstrate the Supreme Court's conviction that "NEPA cannot serve as the basis for a substantial revision of the carefully constructed procedural specifications of the APA."[13] In other words, the rulemaking procedures mandated by the APA continued to serve as the maximum requirements, NEPA notwithstanding.

The major thrust of the Rehnquist opinion was a rebuke of the Court of Appeals for usurping the agency's control over its own rulemaking functions. He argued that "the court improperly intruded into the agency's decisionmaking process."[14] He pointed out that "for more than four decades" the Supreme Court has sought to restrain the lower courts from judicial intervention in the administrative agencies' right to formulate their own procedures.[15] The Supreme Court has guarded the rights of the administrative agencies because they were established by Congress for the purposes of regulation, and Rehnquist emphasized that it was the intent of Congress that these agencies do the regulating, rather than the courts: "Congress intended that the discretion of the *agencies* and not of the courts . . . be exercised . . . . "[16]

Having justified his decision with both judicial precedent and statutory intent, Rehnquist next asserted that his interpretation of the law could also be defended on the basis of good judgment. He pointed out the advantages of administrative agencies' jurisdiction over their own rule. He stated first that the impact of judicial review on administrative law was apt to be "totally unpredictable."[17] Secondly, he said "the inherent advantages of informal rulemaking would be totally lost"[18] because the threat of judicial review would force agencies to conduct full adjudicatory hearings in every instance.

While the Supreme Court criticized Chief Judge Bazelon's interference with Commission rulemaking procedures, it did not validate the Fuel Cycle Rule of 1974. Apparently, Rehnquist shared the Court of Appeals' apprehension that Dr. Pittman's testimony had been inadequately documented. He noted that NEPA intended "to insure a fully informed and well-considered decision."[19] Rehnquist remanded the Rule to the Commission so that it could elaborate on its initial decision, without augmenting its previous procedural format.[20]

The second issue on which the Supreme Court ruled was the question of energy conservation. The Court of Appeals had remanded the Midland plant construction permit to the Commission for reconsideration of the possibility of using conservation alternatives to avoid the need for the nuclear plant's electricity, but the Supreme Court reversed this ruling. Rehnquist noted that it is the province of state public utility commissions and the Federal Power Commission to analyze the projected need for electricity, and they had agreed with the Consumers Power demand forecast in regard to the need for the Midland plant. The primary concern of the Commission, according to its statutory responsibility, remains public health and safety.

Rehnquist said that NEPA has "altered slightly the statutory balance"[21] by mandating the consideration of alternatives to any proposed action in environmental impact statements. However, the Court ruled that the consideration of alternatives "must be bounded by some notion of feasibility" and is not expected to include every possibility "conceivable by the mind of man."[22] Rehnquist enjoined a "common sense" approach because "time and resources are simply too limited to hold that an impact statement fails because the agency failed to ferret out every possible alternative, regardless of how uncommon or unknown . . . . ."[23]

What particularly motivated the Supreme Court to reverse the lower court in regard to conservation was the judicial hindsight evident in its opinion. Rehnquist held that the "concept of 'alternatives' is an evolving one,"[24] and it was only fair to judge the Commission licensing decision on the basis of the information that was available to the ASLB at the time that the construction permit was granted. He cautioned against retroactively applying later standards and information to earlier decisions, calling it "Monday morning quarterbacking."[25]

While the Court of Appeals had criticized the agency for its "threshhold test" and the consequent burden put on the intervenors to explain their contentions, the Supreme Court agreed with the Commission's perspective. Rehnquist alerted intervenors that the Supreme Court expected them to make their participation in agency hearings "meaningful." In a forceful criticism of the Saginaw Intervenors' involvement in the licensing process, the Court admonished:

> Indeed, administrative proceedings should not be a game or a forum to engage in unjustified obstructionism by making cryptic and obscure reference to matters that 'ought to be' considered and then, after failing to do more to bring the matter to the agency's attention, seeking to have that agency determination vacated on the ground that the agency failed to consider matters 'forcefully presented'.[26]

The Supreme Court again instructed the Court of Appeals that its role in reviewing agency decisions was limited and that judicial judgment should not be substituted for administrative judgment.[27]

In regard to the intervenors' contention that Dow Chemical Company had changed its mind about the need for process steam from the Midland plant, the Supreme Court refused to involve itself in the matter. The Rehnquist opinion said that the matter had already been reconsidered and dismissed by the Commission, and the Court believed that the agency had acted properly.[28]

The final matter on which the Supreme Court struck down the Court of Appeals ruling concerned the Advisory Committee on Reactor Safeguards (ACRS) report for the Midland nuclear plant. The lower court had remanded the report to the ACRS for "further elaboration, understandable to a layman, of the reference to other problems."[29] The Supreme Court here again rebuked the Court of Appeals for having "unjustifiably intruded into the administrative process."[30]

The Rehnquist opinion stated that Congress had intended two functions for the ACRS: first, provision of technical advice to the Commission, and, secondly, public statement of the ACRS position regarding the safety of each proposed nuclear plant. The Court ruled that the latter function was secondary to the former one, with no congressional mandate that the public report be a "full technical exposition of every facet of nuclear energy."[31] Furthermore, the Court noted that ACRS reports and documents are routinely on file for observation in the Commission's public documents room.

At this point, the Rehnquist opinion sympathetically elucidated the tribulations of Consumers Power Company in its pursuit of a construction permit for the Midland plant. He cited the fact that the reports filed for the permit "literally fill books," "the proceedings took years," and "the actual hearings themselves [took]) over two weeks."[32] Rehnquist characterized as "Kafkaesque" the Court of Appeals nullification of this "exhaustive proceeding" for "a single alleged oversight on a peripheral issue."[33] He suggested that the judges of the lower court themselves might oppose the development of nuclear energy but that their unhappiness with the result of the licensing decision did not warrant their judicial intrusion into the administrative process.

In conclusion, the Supreme Court transferred the burden of decision making regarding the future of nuclear energy away from the courts and back to Congress. Rehnquist pointed out that the legislative body must have been aware of the criticisms of atomic energy and the unsolved waste disposal problems but had not altered its commitment to the development of nuclear power. The courts should not interfere with this policymaking function: "Nuclear energy may some day be a cheap, safe source of power or it may not. But Congress has made a choice to at least try nuclear energy, establishing a reasonable review process in which courts are to play only a limited role."[34]

Influences on the Supreme Court Ruling

It was demonstrated in chapter 6 that the environmental groups' decision to file suit in the sympathetic D.C. Circuit worked to their advantage in helping to bring about a favorable judicial ruling. However, when the Midland opinion was appealed to the Supreme Court, the fact that it had come from the D.C. Circuit became more advantageous to the nuclear industry.

There are several reasons why the Supreme Court may accept a writ of *certiorari,* the three most important being conflict among the lower courts, a case of general significance, or the perception of an error in a lower court's ruling. The Supreme Court's ruling on the Midland case states quite clearly which of the reasons accounts for the acceptance of the utilities' writ of certiorari:

> We granted certiorari to review two judgments of the Court of Appeals for the District of Columbia Circuit because of our concern that they had seriously misread or misapplied this statutory and decisional law cautioning reviewing courts against engrafting their own notions of proper procedures upon agencies entrusted with substantive functions by Congress.[35]

In other words, the Court of Appeals ruling was at odds with the policy of judicial restraint which the Burger Court had been prescribing for the lower courts.

The Midland case ruling was characteristic of the Burger Court's efforts to delineate and constrict the federal judiciary's jurisdictional boundaries. The Supreme Court for several years has been making frequent rulings that take the policymaking burden off the courts and put it instead on the shoulders of Congress or the states. Use of state courts has been encouraged; controversial policy issues have been avoided; and activist judges have been restrained.[36] This combination of legislative deference and attention to federalism was clearly evident in one of the closing statements of the Midland opinion: "Time may prove wrong the decision to develop nuclear energy, but it is Congress or the States within their appropriate agencies which must eventually make that judgment."[37]

The Supreme Court is regularly faced with appeals of lower court rulings in which it can choose to grant certiorari and overturn activist appeals courts. Many of these cases would serve as well as the Midland case as a forum for the Burger Court to lecture on the value of judicial restraint. Furthermore, the majority of the Supreme Court's grants of certiorari in cases involving a federal agency occur when the Justice Department has brought a case to its attention and advised that it be heard. Therefore, it is especially surprising that the Midland case was selected because the Justice Department had specifically informed the Supreme Court that the case was not significant enough to merit its review.

The explanation for the Supreme Court's review of the Midland case in particular can be found in its opinion. Besides believing that the Court of Appeals had wrongly exercised judicial intervention in Commission procedures, the Supreme Court said that it considered the case worthy of review because of its precedent-setting impact. The Rehnquist opinion noted that "the vast majority of challenges to administrative agency action are brought to the Court of Appeals for the District of Columbia Circuit."[38] In fact, one-fifth of the total number of administrative law cases are heard by the D.C. Circuit, so the Supreme Court was especially eager to influence that Circuit's approach to administrative law.[39]

As noted in chapter 6, the D.C. Circuit has long had a reputation for sympathizing with consumer and environmental groups, as well as for remanding administrative agency rulings on procedural grounds. Furthermore, that Circuit is regarded as a particularly distinguished appellate court so that its rulings are especially apt to set precedents for other federal courts. The D.C. Circuit has sometimes been labeled the "Mini Supreme Court."[40] Therefore, it is the degree of influence that the D.C. Circuit has on judicial precedents that makes its decisions especially susceptible to scrutiny by the Supreme Court. The frequent Supreme Court review of D.C. Circuit opinions coupled with the current difference in judicial philosophies, in combination, lead to a high percentage of that Circuit's rulings being eventually overturned.[41] It is evident, therefore, that the advantage that the antinuclear Saginaw Intervenors gained by initially filing suit in the sympathetic D.C. Circuit instead of another court of appeals worked to their disadvantage when the case was appealed to the Supreme Court. Had the Midland case originally been heard in another circuit, there probably would have been less chance that the Burger Court would have granted certiorari.

A second potential influence on the outcome of the Midland and Vermont Yankee cases in the Supreme Court, in addition to the reputation of the Court of Appeals, was the quantity of party and friend-of-the-court briefs. The parties involved in the litigation had the support of a broad segment of their respective national interest groups. Friend-of-the-court (amici curiae) briefs are considerably more common in Supreme Court cases than in lower appellate court cases; and there were six new friends-of-the-court involved here, representing a large number of organizations, utilities, and state governments. According to the litigants in the Midland case, however, none of these supporting briefs were solicited. The parties did give their permission for the briefs to be filed, but no effort was made by either the environmental groups or the utility to organize or coordinate the legal points that would be raised in the friend-of-the-court briefs.[42]

Nonetheless, the positions of the parties and the friends-of-the-court on the opposing sides of the Supreme Court litigation were cohesive and consistent in the way they framed the legal questions for the Court. While the nuclear industry and its supporters argued that the duration and complexity of the nuclear plant licensing process was already adequate, the environmental groups and their supporters argued that additional procedural safeguards were important to protect the public from the dangers of nuclear power. While the nuclear industry warned that allowing the Court of Appeals ruling to stand would deal a further crippling blow to atomic power, the environmental groups pointed out that the ruling had not yet stopped either the construction or operation of a single nuclear plant. Both sides of the questions were well articulated.

The nuclear industry especially benefited from the support of the Solicitor General who was representing the government as a respondent in the case.[43] The importance of his brief is evidenced by the fact that the Supreme Court opinion directly incorporated from it some ideas and a quotation. When the Supreme Court had first agreed to hear the Midland case, the Solicitor General's position was uncertain. Although the utilities and the Commission had sided together when the Commission was the respondent in the Court of Appeals case, the utilities were unsure about whether the Solicitor General would choose to align himself with them when they became the petitioners in the Supreme Court. In fact, the Justice Department had specifically asked the Court not to grant the writ of certiorari, saying that the case was not sufficiently important to concern the Court. Furthermore, the Justice Department had argued in its original memorandum to the Supreme Court concerning certiorari that the Court of Appeals ruling was sound. Later, when the Justice Department filed its brief in support of the utilities, the Supreme Court commented that the government had been "Janus-like" in taking both positions and changing sides "as nimbly as if dancing a quadrille."[44]

The Solicitor General's original indecision on the case may have been related to the ambiguity of President Carter's own position on nuclear power since the President appoints the Solicitor General himself and, naturally, tries to choose someone with a similar ideological and judicial point of view. However, Wade McCree, Jr., Carter's Solicitor General, has been known for his independent decision making and says that he "never gets White House instructions on what position the government should take in court appearances."[45] Nonetheless, he does try to make his briefs consistent with other Executive branch policies, as evidenced by his referral in the

Midland case to an Executive Order issued to the Council on Environmental Quality. That order told the Council to reduce their paperwork, focus on real environmental problems, and make environmental impact statements as concise as possible.[46] McCree's brief concluded, therefore, that the Supreme Court should overturn the Court of Appeals' instructions to the Commission to extend its rulemaking requirements.

There was undoubtedly great value to the utilities in having the Solicitor General on their side. His office has long been known for its close ties and special relationship with the Supreme Court. Since his staff is familiar with recent government cases and points of law that have influenced the Court, the Solicitor General's brief is apt to be very influential. His reputation for impartiality, even on cases involving the government as a party, also contributes to the Supreme Court's high regard for his opinion. As a result, the government has won 64 percent of the Supreme Court cases in which it has been a party and 87 percent of the cases in which it has been a friend-of-the-court.[47] The interest group with the support of the Solicitor General, therefore, goes into the Supreme Court with an advantage. Had McCree not filed a brief on behalf of the utilities and the Commission in the Midland and Vermont Yankee cases, the Supreme Court would have concluded that he still did not support them, as he had not supported their petition for a writ of certiorari. As one observer has noted, "Although not quite the kiss of death—the agencies sometimes win in these circumstances—this kind of handicap certainly does not help them."[48]

In addition to the Solicitor General's brief and the briefs from Consumers Power and the Vermont Yankee Nuclear Power Corporation, the nuclear industry had the backing of two coalitions of utilities. Baltimore Gas and Electric Company and fourteen other utilities had participated in the Commission's rulemaking on waste disposal and became respondents in the case that went before the Court of Appeals. They then filed a brief regarding waste disposal in support of the petitioning utilities on appeal to the Supreme Court. Probably as a result of several trade association meetings to discuss the Court of Appeals ruling in 1976, Edison Electric Institute, the electric utility trade association, filed its own friend-of-the-court brief on waste disposal in coordination with six utilities which had done the same thing for the original case. Just as Dow Chemical Company had declined to participate in the Court of Appeals litigation, it did not submit a brief on behalf of Consumers Power for the Supreme Court either.

Two nonprofit public interest groups that engage in legal advocacy to support atomic energy submitted briefs on behalf of the nuclear industry. The Pacific Legal Foundation supported Vermont Yankee and the Commission on the waste disposal issue. In regard to the Midland case specifically, a brief was submitted jointly by Scientists and Engineers for Secure

Energy (Hans Bethe, et al.) and the Mid-America Legal Foundation of Chicago, one of eight branches of the consortium called the National Legal Center for the Public Interest in Washington. A third brief was filed by the United States Labor Party, saying that it has many members in the Midland, Michigan area.

In support of the antinuclear groups, the Union of Concerned Scientists submitted a friend-of-the-court brief on the waste disposal question. Another brief came from a coalition of twenty-four states incorporating the ideas of both Kansas and New York in the Court of Appeals case regarding nuclear waste. In spite of the friend-of-the-court briefs on behalf of both the environmental groups and the nuclear industry, however, it was the Solicitor General's position in support of the utilities that probably had the greatest impact on the Supreme Court ruling.

Another potential influence on the Supreme Court decision in the Midland case was current legal scholarship. Law reviews often serve as listening posts for the judiciary since their articles help the judges gauge public reaction to specific lower court rulings.[49] The Court was probably aware of the considerable commentary in the law reviews on the Bazelon opinions in the Midland and Vermont Yankee cases, even though none of these articles were written by any of the parties directly involved in the litigation. An examination of the law reviews shows that nuclear power advocates bemoaned the Bazelon rulings while nuclear opponents applauded them. However, there was not a single article in the journals that fully endorsed all aspects of the Court of Appeals opinions. All of the commentary contained some criticism of the appellate court's ruling.

An article in the *Georgetown Law Journal* expressed satisfaction that the Court had subjected the question of nuclear waste disposal to judicial review but commented that Bazelon's prescriptions for rulemaking were too "broad and ambiguous."[50] Similarly, the *DePaul Law Review* was enthusiastic about the court's oversight of the Commission but said that unfortunately the court "did not give much direction to agencies for future rulemaking."[51] The *Minnesota Law Review* agreed with the Court of Appeals' mandate to the Commission for more informed decision making. However, it felt that the ruling would only serve to increase the expense and delay involved in administrative procedures so that the "small benefits (which) might accrue from *Aeschliman* are likely to be outweighed by their costs."[52]

Those who favored the continued development of nuclear power were even more critical of the Bazelon ruling. Two lawyers who practice before the Commission and often represent the utilities in court commented that the Court of Appeals opinion ignored congressional statutory intent and did not "lend decisional recognition to the energy policy which currently exists."[53] An article in the *University of Pennsylvania Law Review* charged that Chief Judge Bazelon's prescription for hybrid rulemaking in the Commission was simply a "judicial creation of the District of Columbia Circuit."[54]

Perhaps because of all the negative comment on his rulings, Chief Judge Bazelon himself twice gave lectures in the succeeding year that were later published in law reviews. These lectures mentioned the criticisms that were being made of the Midland and Vermont Yankee opinions, noting that "my dissenting colleagues have sometimes seen, in my own opinions, a substantive message wrapped in a procedural envelope."[55]

Rather than expounding on his decisions, Bazelon expressed his own discomfort with the burden that the courts were being asked to assume in regard to administrative procedures. Reiterating his concern about his lack of scientific expertise in matters such as nuclear power, Bazelon discussed the proposal to set up a separate Science Court that would devote itself to the judicial review of technical subjects. He explained, however, his conviction that "many supposedly scientific or technical decisions involve painful value choices" that should not be "the exclusive domain of the scientists and engineers."[56] Bazelon noted defensively that it was the responsibility of political leaders to start making the policy choices and said he regretted that the courts had become the forum for scientific value judgments.

Although all the law review articles, even those by Chief Judge Bazelon, questioned the Court of Appeals decisions, the only article that can be positively cited as an influence on the Supreme Court opinion is the one actually footnoted in Rehnquist's text:[57] namely, Skelly Wright's article in the *Cornell Law Review* entitled "The Courts and the Rulemaking Process: The Limits of Judicial Review." It concerned judicial review of administrative procedures and asserted that excessive judicial involvement would lead to unpredictability and "administrative paralysis."[58] A quotation from Wright's article containing these assertions had also appeared in the Solicitor General's brief,[59] thereby confirming the influence that the brief probably had on Rehnquist in writing his opinion.

The Supreme Court's Midland ruling exemplified its predilection for judicial restraint and acceptance of the policies made by the other branches of government. The Burger Court has appeared to agree with scholarly criticism of the Warren Court's activism. Just prior to the Midland decision, two of the most outstanding judicial scholars published books that recommended a renewed emphasis on judicial restraint.

In 1976, Archibald Cox's *The Role of the Supreme Court in American Government* admonished the courts to stop making "public policy under the doctrine of judicial review."[60] While agreeing with the wisdom and fairness of the Warren Court's decisions, Cox said that the policymaking should be done by Congress. He pointed out that the "courts control neither the purse nor the sword,"[61] thereby explaining the judiciary's reliance on the executive and legislative branches of government for the enforcement of its rulings. Cox was echoing the remark that President Andrew Jackson was supposed to have made when he disagreed with a Supreme Court decision: "Chief Justice Marshall has made his decision; now let him enforce it."

In advising against judicial policymaking, Cox was warning the courts not to sacrifice their "power of legitimacy," their "power to command acceptance and support from the community so as to render force unnecessary." Cox cautioned that judicial activism could potentially make the courts "vulnerable to assaults and reprisals."[62]

A similar warning was expressed in the fall of 1977, just prior to the Midland case argument, in Raoul Berger's *Government by Judiciary: The Transformation of the Fourteenth Amendment.* Though his subject was the use of the Fourteenth Amendment to desegregate and liberalize suffrage, his theme was also judicial restraint in order to preserve "public respect for the Court."[63] Berger wrote:

> Among the most fundamental (Constitutional principles) is the exclusion of the judiciary from policymaking . . . . How long can public respect for the Court, on which its power ultimately depends, survive if the people become aware that the tribunal which condemns the actions of others as unconstitutional is itself acting unconstitutionally?[64]

Thus, the Supreme Court ruling on the Midland case reflected the influence of scholarly disenchantment with judicial activism, as well as the law reviews' criticisms of the Court of Appeals.

An additional influence on judicial decision making is the tenor of public opinion, and the Supreme Court ruling addressed itself to the justices' perception of the public. Rehnquist instructed the Court of Appeals not "to impose upon the agency its own notion of which procedures are 'best' or most likely to further some vague, undefined public good."[65] Similarly, in rejecting the intervenors' charge that the public had not understood the ACRS report, the Court said that "not one member of the supposedly uncomprehending public even asked that the report be remanded."[66] Just as the Court of Appeals opinion indicated that the public should be protected from nuclear power, so the Supreme Court ruled that it was the responsibility of Congress and the states to make public policy.

By the time that the Supreme Court ruling was handed down in the Midland and Vermont Yankee cases, the nuclear controversy had become one of the most polarized public opinion issues, evoking bitterness and, on occasion, civil disobedience. Perhaps the intensity of the national controversy accounts for the unanimity of the Court's decision in this case since the justices tend to avoid divisions in "threat situations" in which criticism and backlash are possible. As David Rohde and Harold Spaeth explain:

Normally, the Court forms minimum winning opinion coalitions (5 to 4, 5 to 3, 4 to 3) except when the justices perceive noncompliance with the Court's decision to be likely . . . . In the face of such threats, instead of forming a minimum winning coalition, the Court's decision tends to be unanimous, with all the participating justices concurring in a single opinion.[67]

In addition to public opinion, media coverage of legal controversies sometimes influences judicial rulings. In regard to media influence on the Supreme Court, the opinion in the Midland case did not cite specific articles, as the Court of Appeals ruling had done. Furthermore, media coverage of nuclear power controversies had become so frequent and extensive that it would be difficult to single out any particular newspaper or magazine articles that might have influenced the Court or to prove that they were instigated by the parties to the Midland case.

It should be noted, however, that there were two articles on Midland, both with wide circulation, that were published in the three months prior to the oral argument in the Supreme Court and were sympathetic to the environmentalists. The first appeared in August, 1977, in Jack Anderson's syndicated column in many newspapers across the country, including the *Washington Post*. It concerned the contractual disagreements between Consumers Power and Dow Chemical Company over the Midland nuclear plant. The contract between the two companies that was renegotiated in 1974 had first become an issue during the hearing of the Midland case in the Court of Appeals.

After the Court of Appeals ruling in 1976, the relationship between the two companies had deteriorated further. The Commission's decision to convene a new ASLB to again review the Midland plant's construction permit had made the Dow Company more apprehensive about the prospects of ever seeing the plant completed. Dow needed the steam and electricity from the nuclear plant as quickly as possible to replace the use of its outdated coal–fired plant. Dow began to regret its involvement in the Midland plant that was taking years longer to complete than had originally been anticipated.

A letter from Joseph Temple, then chief of the Midland division of Dow, to Paul Oreffice, President of Dow Chemical USA, specifically stated that Dow would be better off without the contract for the long–delayed nuclear plant. Consumers Power reacted by threatening Dow with a $600 million lawsuit if it reneged on its contract for process steam. Myron Cherry, the Saginaw Intervenors' lawyer, then brought this dispute to the attention of the new ASLB reviewing Midland's construction permit in the fall of 1976.

A year later, and just prior to the ASLB's ruling on whether to halt further construction pending the outcome of the Supreme Court decision, the Jack Anderson column appeared. Its timing and contents made it appear to have been instigated by the Midland intervenors to affect the ASLB. Anderson accused Consumers Power of involvement in a "corporate Watergate" in which "the giant utility . . . allegedly has tried to prevent witnesses from giving information to federal investigators, has laundered testimony [before the ASLB] that might be damaging and has given the regulatory tribunal incomplete information."[68] The ASLB ruling in September, 1977, allowed the Midland plant construction to continue in spite of the allegations; and although the Supreme Court questioned Consumers Power carefully about the Dow relationship during the oral argument, the Court did not involve itself in the problem.

A second article on the Midland plant appeared in the September, 1977, issue of *Audubon*. Entitled "The Outrageous Mr. Cherry and the Underachieving Nukes," it described Myron Cherry and Mary Sinclair as "crusaders" and nuclear power plants as "an accident waiting to happen."[69] It included a lengthy and comprehensive description of the Midland controversy from the intervenors' point of view.

Just prior to the issuance of the Supreme Court ruling on Midland, an article on the case appeared on the front page of the *Wall Street Journal*. Entitled "Using the Law's Delay, Myron Cherry Attacks Atomic Power Projects," the article chronicled Cherry's successful career as an antinuclear lawyer. It pointed out that he had been able to extend the hearings process for the Midland construction permit and that his strategy consisted of wearing down the utilities through years of expensive litigation. As a result, John Selby, the President of Consumers Power, was reported to regret having ever begun the Midland plant and to have said, "I'd be very reluctant to put shareholders' money into another nuclear plant in the future."[70] The article concluded, therefore, that " . . . as Mr. Cherry loses battle after battle, he just may, as Mr. Selby's remarks indicate, be slowly winning the war."[71] In regard to the influence of the article on the Court, one commentator said, "It could be Mr. Cherry outsmarted himself, that his revealing remarks had something to do with the Supreme Court ruling."[72] In any case, the Rehnquist opinion certainly responded to the theme of the article by holding that the courts should not further extend the "exhaustive proceeding" and should "play only a limited role" in the nuclear power licensing process.[73]

Summary and Conclusions

Because the Commission did not appeal the unfavorable Court of Appeals ruling on the Midland and Vermont Yankee nuclear plants, the two utilities decided to use legal advocacy and petition the Supreme Court for a writ of certiorari themselves. The Supreme Court agreed to hear the two cases jointly. In a unanimous ruling, the Court overturned the lower court's opinion and reinstated the Midland construction permit and the Vermont Yankee operating license. Although the fuel cycle or radioactive waste disposal rule was remanded to the Commission and the Court of Appeals for further elucidation, that remand no longer directly jeopardized the construction of the Midland plant.

Just as the environmental groups and the nuclear industry had done little to actively influence the nature of the Court of Appeals ruling, so the same interest groups largely refrained from the use of traditional group tactics to influence the Supreme Court's judicial policymaking process. Although three media articles on Midland were published prior to the Court's ruling, there is no direct correlation visible between the groups' strategy regarding the litigation and the articles' publication; nor is there any direct causal relationship between their publication and the Court's decision.

The Supreme Court was probably influenced to a greater extent by its perception of the activist nature of the D.C. Circuit, which went counter to the judicial restraint practiced by the Burger Court. The publication of legal scholarship that was critical of judicial intervention in administrative decision making and of the Bazelon rulings in particular may have contributed to the Court's decision. Although there were many unsolicited friend–of–the–court briefs for both parties to the Midland case, the Solicitor General's position as a respondent supporting the nuclear industry was what seemed to play an obvious role in shaping the nature of the Rehnquist ruling. Thus, it may be concluded that factors other than direct interest group influences on the Supreme Court were the primary determinants of its judicial policymaking regarding the Midland nuclear plant.

8 The Impact of the Judicial Ruling

In its opinion on the Midland atomic plant, the Supreme Court had dismissed the antinuclear groups' charges and ruled that the plant could be completed. Thus, the environmental groups' immediate objective of curtailing construction had been thwarted by the judicial opinion, and one would expect that the setback would weaken their organization and resources. It would also seem that the definitive Supreme Court ruling favorable to the nuclear industry would bolster its position, and the Court's mandate regarding the Midland plant would expedite the Commission's regulatory and licensing process.

This chapter will examine the impact of the judicial policymaking on the Commission and the interest groups involved specifically in the Midland plant controversy. The Court's policy output, that is, the content of the judicial opinion itself, will be contrasted with the policy impact of the judicial process.

The Effect of the Ruling on the Commission

The Supreme Court had unequivocally approved both the Commission's issuance of a construction permit for the nuclear plant and also the Commission's legislative procedures for rulemaking. Having won its court case, the Commission's licensing procedures in regard to Midland seemed to be largely vindicated. Marcus Rowden, the former chairman of the Commission, expressed relief that the Court had given the agency such "sound ground rules" to direct its future procedural decisions.[1] It seemed as if judicial review had in this case produced clear guidelines for the Commission.

However, the Commission continued its intensive regulatory involvement with the Midland plant. The Atomic Safety and Licensing Board (ASLB) hearings on the remanded Midland construction permit were still open when the Supreme Court issued its ruling in April, 1978; and, as of the spring of 1979, the Commission had not yet brought them to a conclusion. The Supreme Court had ruled out the need for further discussion of the waste disposal rule, the Advisory Committee on Reactor Safeguards (ACRS) report, or the conservation issue; but the Commission still wanted to investigate the possible impropriety of Consumers Power's influence on Dow Chemical Company witnesses regarding their testimony concerning the rift between the two companies (see chapter 7).

In order to explain the full extent of Commission involvement at Midland, it should be noted that there were two other major regulatory issues, besides the construction permit issuance, that had arisen in regard to the nuclear plant. One of these concerned quality assurance standards. After initially granting the construction permit for Midland in 1972, the Commission retroactively issued an amendment to all its construction permits in May, 1973, incorporating quality assurance reporting requirements. A subsequent inspection of the Midland construction site in November, 1973, found deficiences in its welding of concrete reinforcing steel. As a result, the Commission issued a sharp reprimand to Consumers Power and a Show Cause order, asking the utility to show why construction should not be suspended pending a determination that the company was in full compliance with the quality assurance regulations. To investigate the company's compliance, a show cause hearing began in Midland in July, 1974. The ASLB issued its findings in September, 1974, saying that Consumers Power's quality assurance then complied with Commission regulations.

The second major issue, in addition to the construction permit issuance, in which the Commission involved itself was a possible violation of antitrust laws by Consumers Power Company in regard to the plant. Although the first Atomic Safety and Licensing Board (ASLB) had originally ruled that Consumers Power could have sole ownership of the nuclear plant, a later Appeal Board decided on December 30, 1977, that Consumers Power would be required to sell a part of the plant to other small Michigan utilities that might wish access to nuclear power.

Besides the problems peculiar to the Midland plant, there was continued uncertainty for Consumers Power Company and the rest of the nuclear industry regarding the issue of radioactive waste disposal. The Commission extended its interim rule on waste management until the adoption of a final rule in August, 1979. Nevertheless, the Midland and Vermont Yankee cases remained open on the docket of the Court of Appeals pending the resolution of further appeals of the rulemaking by the environmentalists.

The blame for the indecision and inertia regarding nuclear plant licensing and radioactive waste disposal should go less to the Commission, the institution charged with the application of statutes, than to Congress, the institution empowered with the authority to make nuclear power policy. In 1978 Congress did begin to rethink its mandates regarding nuclear energy policy. After six months of drafts, President Carter sent his Nuclear Licensing Reform Bill to Congress. However, the bill was stalled in congressional committee sessions at the end of 1978, and the Three Mile Island nuclear plant accident in the spring of 1979 generated considerable discussion in Congress regarding nuclear plant licensing requirements. As for the question of managing radioactive waste disposal, Congress enacted no policy or program. In 1979, the nuclear industry was still urging the Carter administration to commit itself to a waste disposal demonstration program, but no action was taken.

As Justice Rehnquist had stated in the Midland opinion, "Time may prove wrong the decision to develop nuclear energy, but it is Congress or the States within their appropriate agencies which must eventually make that judgment."[2] Without congressional action, the Commission remained in a state of paralysis. There seemed to be no final resolution in sight of any of the questions surrounding the Midland plant specifically or the development of nuclear power in general.

The Effect of the Ruling on the Environmentalists

There initially appeared to be a real winner and a real loser in the Supreme Court ruling on Midland, and the equilibrium between the interest groups seemed to shift. Ostensibly, the environmental groups had lost their court suit. Mary Sinclair, the leader of the Saginaw Intervenors, reacted glumly to the Court's definitive opinion by saying that she would not pursue further legal action against the Midland plant. She charged, "In a way, the Supreme Court is like Pontius Pilate, washing its hands of issues with such impact."[3]

The initial concern of the environmental groups was the effect of the litigation on their resources. In January, 1978, Myron Cherry, the Saginaw Intervenors' attorney, announced his intention to sue the Mapleton Intervenors for about $116,000 for having represented their interests in the Court of Appeals. The Mapleton group reacted angrily to Cherry's threatened suit. They claimed that the Court of Appeals had insisted on the unification of the Saginaw and Mapleton Intervenors' suits against the nuclear plant and that they had already paid Cherry $37,000 for his time and would pay him no more.[4]

Then, to add to the environmental groups' financial concerns, the Supreme Court awarded the court costs to the utilities, to be paid by the environmental groups as the losing parties in the lawsuit. The court costs were $51,600, of which $300 was owed to the clerk of the Supreme Court and $51,300 was the cost of printing the record of the case for the Supreme Court. The huge printing bill resulted from the fact that the years of licensing hearings and regulatory involvement had produced many volumes of records. The Natural Resources Defense Council (NRDC) and the New England Coalition on Nuclear Pollution were ordered to pay $15,000 to Vermont Yankee Nuclear Power Corporation and a utility coalition, and they probably did comply with the ruling. In the Midland case, the Supreme Court assessed the Saginaw Intervenors $20,000 to be paid to Consumers

Power Company. The Supreme Court did not assess the remaining portion of the bill for court costs.

The Supreme Court's decision to award court costs came as a surprise to the parties in the case. The environmentalists believed that similar organizations which had lost Supreme Court suits had usually not been asked to pay court costs at all. However, if the fees were assessed, the environmentalists expected them not to amount to more than $2,000 at the most.[5] The Court has no specific rules regarding cost assessments, and the procedures by which the decision was made were unclear. The cost assessment message arrived without explanation from the clerk's office over a month after the Court's decision was handed down, and the Supreme Court did not tell the utilities how they should collect the fees.

Although Consumers Power was briefly uncertain about whether to collect payment, the utility did decide to press the Intervenors for the sum. The only two well-funded members of the Saginaw Intervenor coalition were the United Auto Workers and the Sierra Club, and both groups took the assessment of court costs very seriously. Even though they had done little more than lend their names to the intervention, their position as the most "collectible" of the organizations made them the most likely to have to shoulder the financial burden. Consequently, they petitioned the Supreme Court to reduce or eliminate the cost assessment, but the Court denied the request. It was not until Consumers Power filed a collection suit in the Midland County Circuit Court in May, 1979, that the Intervenors began to comply with the Supreme Court's ruling. By June, the UAW had paid the utility $10,000, the Sierra Club had paid $5,000, and the West Michigan Environmental Action Council had paid $3,300. Consumers Power continued to press Mary Sinclair and her fellow intervenors for the remaining $1,700.[6] Mary Sinclair had previously announced that her Saginaw Valley Nuclear Study Group was defunct and that, furthermore, she would rather go to jail than pay the court costs.[7] However, she eventually complied with the court ruling, and Consumers Power collected the full amount.

After the Supreme Court ruling, the capability of the environmental groups was not only threatened by financial strain but also by the potential loss of Myron Cherry as their attorney. Cherry's style in the Commission hearings had been characterized by abrasive, aggressive behavior, not only toward representatives of the nuclear industry but also toward members of the Commission itself. For instance, Cherry charged that attorneys for the Nuclear Regulatory Commission had distorted the truth and "should be sued by the public for their last two years of pay since they haven't done anything to earn it."[8] Consequently, the Commission's lawyers drew up a formal motion to suspend Cherry from the Midland hearings in January, 1978. A special Atomic Safety and Licensing Board was convened at that time to investigate the charges against Cherry and determine proper attorney conduct at regulatory hearings. Cherry reacted to the Commission's decision with countercharges regarding not only the Midland hearings but also the emergency core cooling system hearings and the Commission's "coverup of the regulatory staff's irresponsibilities."[9] A settlement was eventually reached by the parties involved calling for a blanket withdrawal and dismissal of all charges of misconduct.[10]

Although the capability of the environmental groups was initially undermined by the financial and legal problems, the Supreme Court decision seemed to have no lasting detrimental impact on them. Nuclear opponents reacted to the decision by reorganizing their interest groups into larger units. A coalition of 130,000 people in thirty-five environmental organizations on the East coast formed specifically to address the waste question, calling themselves the Citizens' Project on Radioactive Waste.

In the Midwest, a group called the Great Lakes Energy Alliance met for the first time on May 21, 1978. It was comprised primarily of nuclear opponents from Michigan, and its fight against atomic energy was expected to consist of citizen education, political pressure on politicians, and withholding of electric utility bill payments to protest the construction of nuclear plants. Mary Sinclair, the leader of the Saginaw Intervenors, was also in charge of this new organization. Its members came not only from the ranks of the original environmental groups but were also bolstered by new participants. Some of the Catholic clergymen from the Midland area joined the Great Lakes Energy Alliance with the intention especially of trying to stop the construction of the Midland nuclear plant.[11]

In 1978 and 1979, the Great Lakes Energy Alliance and other antinuclear groups such as the Public Interest Research Group in Michigan (PIRGIM) began to utilize funds provided to them by the Michigan Attorney General's office. The funds had been allocated to the state of Michigan and nine other states by the U.S. Department of Energy through a grant program for the financing of citizen group intervention in regulatory proceedings involving electric rates. Although no federal intervenor funding was specifically provided for nuclear plant licensing hearings, the Alliance and PIRGIM were given $80,000 which they used to intervene in utility rate hearings before the Michigan Public Service Commission.[12] Thanks to the funding, the groups were able to hire experts who contested Consumers Power Company's testimony regarding the economics of its nuclear plants. The environmentalists thereby registered additional protest regarding the utility's construction and operation of atomic plants by challenging its application for a rate hike.

The Three Mile Island accident in March, 1979, further strengthened the Michigan antinuclear groups. Shortly after the accident, an offshoot organization called the Huron Alliance staged an antinuclear march in Midland on April 21, 1979, with 3,500 participants. The protestors pointed out that the Midland plant would be a sister plant of Three Mile Island since both were powered by Babcock and Wilcox pressurized water reactors of the same size and type.

The resurgence of the antinuclear groups was also reinforced by the addition of Michigan's Attorney General Frank J. Kelley to their ranks. Kelley had often intervened in utility rate cases; and he was influenced to oppose the Midland nuclear plant by frequent protests at the plant site, plus "hundreds of telegrams, petitions, letters and calls" from members of the new Great Lakes Energy Alliance.[13] Consequently, Kelly announced on June 5, 1978, that his state agency would intervene in the Commission's public hearings regarding the operating license for the Midland nuclear plant.

Other intervenor petitions were also granted to Wendall Marshall, the leader of the Mapleton Intervenors, and to Mary Sinclair. Mrs. Sinclair would probably be represented again by Myron Cherry. He had previously warned Consumers Power that he would return for the operating license hearings. Said Cherry, "They're never going to get rid of me."[14] Thus, it appeared that the Supreme Court ruling had not seriously undermined the organization or resources of the antinuclear environmental groups. Their capability in mobilizing to oppose the Midland nuclear plant remained effective, as did their resolve.

The Effect of the Ruling on the Nuclear Industry

The Supreme Court decision initially boosted the spirits of the nuclear industry involved in Midland. Consumers Power Company announced that it would now be free to "complete construction of the Midland plant without further threat of delay."[15] Work at the plant site continued at a brisk pace with nearly 3,000 workers employed in June, 1978. The 1976 Court of Appeals decision had not halted or slowed construction anyway because an Atomic Safety and Licensing Board had agreed to allow it to proceed in spite of the remanded hearings. After the Supreme Court ruling, however, the permission to continue construction no longer seemed precarious.

The Supreme Court's endorsement of the construction permit was especially important in bolstering the relationship between Consumers Power and Dow Chemical Company which had floundered after the Court of Appeals decision. On June 27, 1978, after several months of negotiations, the two companies announced a revised contract in which Dow agreed to buy steam from the plant for the first thirty-five years of its operation. Although the Midland plant was expected to begin supplying the steam to Dow in the spring of 1982, Dow was committed to wait for the steam if the plant's operation underwent further delays, at least until December, 1984. Thus, the Rehnquist opinion had encouraged the nuclear industry to believe that the Midland plant would eventually overcome regulatory hurdles and go into operation. However, the extra two and a half years of grace built into the contract by Consumers Power showed that the optimism was somewhat cautious.

The short-term impact of the Supreme Court ruling on nuclear industry optimism was dwarfed by the more significant effect of the duration of the administrative and judicial process regarding the Midland plant. The time previously consumed by the construction, licensing, and start up of Consumers Power's two operating nuclear plants, Big Rock Point and Palisades, had been only three years and five years, respectively. The timetable for Midland was considerably different, however.

Consumers Power had originally announced its intention to build the plant in 1967, and the utility spent one year preparing its application for a construction permit. The public licensing hearings for the plant lasted for two years; and the permit was not issued until 1972, after which the environmental groups appealed the permit to the Atomic Safety and Licensing Appeal Board. When the administrative process was exhausted, the Midland intervenors filed suit against the Commission in the Court of Appeals in 1973; but the court did not hand down its Midland ruling until 1976. The utilities' petition for review of the Midland case finally yielded a decision from the Supreme Court in April, 1978, validating the construction permit.

Meanwhile the cost of the Midland plant had increased. When Consumers Power originally announced its intention to build the plant in 1967, it was scheduled for completion in 1974 and 1975 at an estimated cost of $349 million. By the time the Supreme Court handed down its decision, the plant's operation had been postponed until 1981 and 1982, and the plant cost was $1.67 billion and rising.

The Midland plant's construction delays and cost increases could be partially attributed to factors that affected all nuclear plants under construction in the early 1970s and were unrelated to the environmental groups' intervention in the administrative hearings and initiation of litigation. Consumers Power determined the various reasons for budget changes by breaking them down into several major categories: time-related increases (cost of money over an extended period); changing regulatory requirement and code changes (that is, the costs directly attributable to changes in regulations and codes and in their interpretation by regulatory agencies, beyond those in effect when the original estimate was made); increases due to project evolution, scope changes and job experience (including design modifications and improved understanding of materials and labor productivity); and construction permit delays, suspensions, and extended schedule (that is, time losses related to the duration of the administrative licensing process, the new regulatory requirements, and financing restrictions). According to Consumers Power, the breakdown of budget cost increases in 1976, by percentages, was as follows:[16]

1. Time Related   27%
2. Changing Regulatory Requirements and Code Changes   16%
3. Project Evolution, Scope Changes and Job Experience   36%
4. Construction Permit Delays, Suspension and Extended Schedule   20%

Thus, almost half of the cost increases, that is, categories I and IV were time–related and could be at least partially attributable to the intervenors' success in adding to the delay in construction from November, 1970, until June, 1973. While it is impossible to put an exact dollar figure on the amount that the environmental groups added to the cost of the plant, it is evident that the increase was several hundred million dollars. Furthermore, the delay in the Midland plant's completion necessitated the construction of two nonnuclear plants to supply the increased demand for electricity, thereby exacerbating Consumers Power Company's own financial strains. Had construction been halted during the Midland litigation, as could have been the case, the expenses to the utility would have been even greater.

After the Supreme Court ruling, the next step in licensing the Midland nuclear plant was to be its operating license hearings. The hearings had been scheduled to begin in 1979, but the Three Mile Island accident caused a delay. The Commission eventually notified Consumers Power Company that there would be at least a year's postponement of the start of its hearings because the Commission staff was busy evaluating the accident and could not deal with the Midland plant for that length of time. Furthermore, since the Midland plant reactor was the same type as the one at Three Mile Island, there would probably be design changes and new regulatory requirements for Midland. Thus, the Three Mile Island incident was certain to add to the duration and expense of the operating license process which could potentially be as lengthy and costly as the ten–year process required to obtain a construction permit.

Through the years of complications with the Midland plant, Consumers Power had not wavered in its belief in the advisability of developing nuclear power as a major energy source. Furthermore, the completion and operation of the Midland plant in particular had assumed increasing urgency for the utility's management because a large share of the company's assets were invested in the plant. For both these reasons, John Selby, the president of Consumers Power, delivered several speeches in 1978 and 1979 as well as testifying before members of Congress about the necessity of allowing the United States to continue to develop the nuclear option for its energy needs. He was convinced that the economic benefits of nuclear power outweighed those of other electric power sources. In regard to Consumers Power, Selby said, "Our studies continue to show that a nuclear plant will generate a kilowatt–hour of electricity about twenty percent cheaper than the next cheapest fuel which is low sulphur Eastern coal."[17] In theory, therefore, the utility remained committed to nuclear power.

In practice, however, the cost of the Midland plant had ruled out the possibility of Consumers Power Company building another atomic plant in the existing regulatory climate. Selby said that even though he believed that nuclear power would be less expensive than other fuels, "the current [regulatory] system places the shareholders and customers at too great a risk."[18] At Midland, $600 million had been invested in the plant before the Supreme Court opinion favoring the utility was handed down. That money might have been lost if the Court had not sanctioned the continuation of the plant's construction. Although Selby made it clear that the utility remained determined to complete and operate the Midland plant, he said that he regretted that it had ever been started.[19]

Summary and Conclusions

It is evident that the policy output from the Supreme Court's judicial ruling on the Midland nuclear plant, that is, the substance of the Court's opinion, differed considerably from the ruling's impact on the interest groups and the Commission. Although the Court had approved the Commission's rule-making procedures, no new waste disposal rule was forthcoming, and Congress continued its inaction regarding resolution of the problem. Furthermore, the Commission's licensing process for the Midland plant was likely to become even more lengthy and indecisive as a result of changing requirements and postponements in the wake of the Three Mile Island nuclear plant accident.

In regard to the Midland environmental groups, the effect of the Supreme Court ruling and assessment of substantial court costs was only a short–term setback. The environmentalists proceeded to reorganize and petition to intervene again in the next stage of the Midland plant's licensing process: its operating license hearings. The construction permit process had been extended for ten years, and the issuance of an operating license would also be contested as long as possible.

As for the nuclear industry, the Court's favorable policy output had initially boosted the industry's morale. However, the Court's ruling did not include any real compensation for the costs of the lengthy regulatory and adjudicatory process at Midland. Furthermore, with the operating license hearings still ahead of it, probably in 1980, Consumers Power Company had already invested over $1 billion in the Midland plant, so there was no turning back. Although the utility intended to persevere in completing the Midland plant, it decided that the economic risk inherent in the construction of nuclear plants had made atomic energy an unviable option for the utility in the future. It may be concluded, then, that although the content of the Supreme Court's policy output regarding the Midland plant favored the nuclear industry, the effect of the litigation process had been the achievement of the environmental groups' long–range objective: an undermining of the utility's commitment to nuclear power.

9 Legal Advocacy and the Nuclear Power Controversy

As evidenced by the decline in utility orders of atomic power plants, the antinuclear environmental groups are clearly winning their battle against atomic energy. The effectiveness of nuclear power's opponents may be attributed, in part, to their group capabilities and strategies. The antinuclear activists especially benefit from the dedication and political skill of their leadership, the full utilization of potential group resources, and the commitment to both traditional and nontraditional political tactics.

Legal advocacy is regarded as one of the nontraditional political tactics, a form of guerrilla warfare in the interest group struggle. Both the environmental groups and the nuclear industry have available to them the legal expertise and funds necessary for litigation. However, it has only been the environmental groups that have taken full advantage of their legal resources by frequently intervening in regulatory hearings and then appealing the Commission's rulings to the courts for judicial review. The nuclear industry, on the other hand, has almost never filed lawsuits to promote the development of atomic energy.

It is important to realize, however, that the success of the environmental groups is a result not only of their political acumen but also of institutional factors over which neither interest group has had much control. The popular image of a David and Goliath scenario obscures the fact that Goliath's impotence stems, in large part, from the governmental regulatory process. Because atomic energy involves a high–risk technology, there are statutory provisions for public participation in its regulation. The licensing procedures for nuclear plants are complex and laborious, allowing intervention and appeals both within the Commission and to the judiciary. The environmental groups take advantage of these access points to exercise influence on bureaucratic policymaking. Furthermore, because the regulatory and adjudicatory processes are lengthy, they can easily be used by the antinuclear groups for the express purpose of causing delay. The environmentalists realize that the delays are very detrimental to the financial stability of the nuclear industry since they add substantially to the costs of the plants whose construction period is extended or whose operation is postponed pending a final ruling. Therefore, legal advocacy is a natural political strategy for the public interest groups which have an adversary relationship with the Commission and want to make nuclear plants prohibitively expensive for the utilities. If Congress passes an intervenor funding bill, there will be further incentives for the use of legal advocacy.[1]

In spite of the fact that the courts have been presented with many atomic energy issues, the judicial opinions themselves have usually disappointed the environmental groups. With the important exception of the Calvert Cliffs case,[2] the judiciary has ordinarily upheld Commission rulings and refrained from active policymaking in regard to the development of nuclear power. However, as demonstrated by the Midland plant case study, the impact of the duration of the judicial process has been as significant as the impact of the actual court rulings. Consequently, the successful nuclear industry litigant has benefited no more than the unsuccessful antinuclear litigants from the judicial opinions. Even though Consumers Power Company won its case in the Supreme Court, the lengthy regulatory hearings and subsequent litigation extended the Midland plant's licensing and, thereby, made nuclear power less economically attractive as an electric energy source for the utility. In fact, in the Midland case, legal advocacy was such an effective interest group strategy for the environmentalists that it has deterred the company from future development of nuclear power plants in the current political climate.[3] Furthermore, Consumers Power Company's decision is representative of similar decisions made by many utilities.[4]

The nuclear industry has, thus far, been unable to counteract the effectiveness of the environmental groups' delaying tactics. Institutional constraints have limited the flexibility of the industry, especially the utilities. As the clientele industry, they are dependent upon the Commission for the issuance of reasonable regulations and timely licenses. This dependent relationship has deterred them from challenging the Commission in court to try to expedite the regulatory process. Furthermore, it is difficult to employ litigation, which is itself a lengthy process, to prevent intervenors' delays. Consequently, for these and other reasons, legal advocacy has, thus far, been used as a political strategy by only one side in the nuclear power controversy. There are indications, however, that the Midland opinion may precipitate a shift in the interest groups' tactics: the nuclear industry may begin to adopt legal advocacy as a strategy, while the environmental groups may use it less frequently.

Even before the Supreme Court's decision, speakers at trade meetings had begun to urge the nuclear industry to start filing lawsuits to defend its interests. For instance, Irving Kristol, speaking at the Edison Electric Institute Convention in 1977, tried to persuade utility executives to try legal advocacy. Kristol pointed out that environmental groups file lawsuits on every conceivable subject in an effort to undermine the utilities. He said that it was time for the utilities to start fighting back by filing suits of their own and then appealing all the unfavorable rulings, as the environmentalists were doing. Kristol predicted that the result of utilities' use of legal advocacy would be more caution and less enthusiasm on the part of their opponents in the legal arena.[5]

The nuclear industry, having been bolstered by the Midland opinion, has been starting to respond to this call for legal advocacy.[6] Since there is a statutory mandate for the federal government to control the development of commercial atomic energy, utilities have begun to sue state and local governments that pass restrictive legislation regarding the development of atomic power. Two such suits, based on the preemption doctrine and challenging California's restrictive legislation, were filed in October, 1978: one by Pacific Gas and Electric and Southern California Edison, and the other by the Pacific Legal Foundation. In addition, the utilities are being encouraged to sue not only the Commission, but also the boards of directors of environmental groups and effective antinuclear lawyers, such as Myron Cherry, for "abuse of process" in the course of public hearings on nuclear power plants.[7]

The newly formed public interest groups that support the development of nuclear power, the Pacific Legal Foundation and the National Legal Center for the Public Interest, are already involved in much litigation. The National Legal Center, for example, has done a survey to identify the major legal problems blocking the development of nuclear power. They have submitted friend-of-the-court briefs on behalf of the nuclear industry in test cases involving these legal obstacles, as was done in the Midland case. These groups have also helped organize other friend-of-the-court briefs, as well as increasingly initiating suits on their own. They believe that they are in a better position to employ legal advocacy than is the nuclear industry itself because they have no fear of reprisal from government agencies or from public opinion, and they can focus on broader issues than any individual corporation in the nuclear industry.[8]

Although the Midland opinion may be serving to precipitate the initiation of litigation by the nuclear industry and its supporters, the impact of the ruling initially included a further withdrawal of the judiciary from involvement in the nuclear controversy. In its Midland opinion, the Supreme Court cautioned the lower courts to engage in judicial restraint and refrain from procedural and substantive intervention in the Commission's rulemaking and licensing.[9] By the end of 1978, the repercussions of that opinion were being felt in the lower courts. For example, in a similar suit, also named *Natural Resources Defense Council* v. *U.S. Nuclear Regulatory Commission,*[10] the environmental groups had again called for a moratorium on nuclear reactor licensing pending solution of the waste disposal problem. Unlike the Vermont Yankee and Midland suits, which were based on the National Environmental Policy Act, this case cited the provisions of the Atomic Energy Act. The U.S. Court of Appeals for the Second Circuit, where the case was heard, did not hand down its ruling until July, 1978. Since the Supreme Court had already ruled on the Midland case by then, it was cited as precedent, saying that the higher court had told the judiciary to stop interfering with the Commission. This trend toward judicial restraint was evident in other 1978 litigation, such as the Supreme Court's ruling in June upholding the constitutionality of the Price–Anderson Act[11] and the First Circuit Court of Appeals' initial rulings in favor of the Nuclear Regulatory Commission's approval of the Seabrook, New Hampshire, nuclear plant in August, 1978.[12]

Because of the judicial setbacks at Midland and elsewhere, it was the opinion of Joseph Sax in 1978 that, for the environmental groups, "the grandeur period of litigation is over."[13] Although his book *Defending the Environment* urged the public interest groups to use legal advocacy in 1971, Sax contended that the courts had already made their substantive interpretations of the National Environmental Policy Act and were generally less interested in environmental matters.[14] Karin Sheldon, an attorney for the New England Coalition on Nuclear Pollution that intervened in the Vermont Yankee case, agreed in 1978 that the antinuclear groups had "come to the end of easy court victories."[15] In addition, the Supreme Court's unexpected assessment of costs to the environmental groups in the Midland case would act as a future deterrent to their frequent use of legal advocacy.[16] Thus, the post–Midland decision climate initially seemed to be one in which legal advocacy was a less effective strategy for the antinuclear groups: the nuclear industry was beginning to initiate its own lawsuits; the judiciary was less sympathetic to the environmentalists' litigation; and the expense of using legal advocacy as a political strategy had risen.

However, time does not stand still in the nuclear power controversy, and the Three Mile Island accident has already altered that post–Midland status quo. Besides leading to an increase in regulatory requirements and licensing postponements for nuclear plants, the accident has also exacerbated public concern regarding the safety of atomic energy. Consequently, legislators are becoming more responsive to antinuclear arguments, and the environmental groups are now focusing their lobbying efforts on state legislatures and, especially, on Congress. A multitude of state and federal legislative bills have been introduced which, if enacted, will further restrict the development of nuclear power.

It is likely that restrictive new legislation will contribute to further use of legal advocacy, perhaps this time by both sets of interest groups. The environmentalists and the nuclear industry can be expected to have differing opinions regarding the proper interpretation and administrative implementation of new statutes, just as has been true of previous nuclear–related legislation. After the statutes have been subjected to interest group contention in the course of Commission hearings, the administrative rulings are likely to be appealed to the courts for judicial review. It is entirely possible, therefore, that the impact of the Three Mile Island accident may nullify the effect of the Midland opinion and contribute to a resurgence of judicial involvement in the nuclear power controversy.

It was long before Three Mile Island that one pronuclear observer of the state of atomic power in this country despaired, "The energy industry today finds itself like the great Gulliver in Lilliput, trussed up by thousands of rules and regulations, by dedicated little zealots who use our overworked legal system to spin their immobilizing web."[17] In the absence of a definitive and generally accepted national energy plan involving the further development of atomic energy, it is unlikely that the legal web will be unraveled to arrest the decline in the development of nuclear power.

Appendix A
Chronology of the Development of the Midland Nuclear Plant

Announcement of the plant.	December 14, 1967
Application for construction permit filed with Atomic Energy Commission (AEC).	January 13, 1969
Beginning of site preparation.	April 15, 1969
Advisory Committee on Reactor Safeguards (ACRS) reports approval of Midland plant design.	June 18, 1970
Construction activity halted during construction permit hearings.	November 14, 1970
Construction permit hearings begin.	December 1, 1970
Atomic Safety and Licensing Board (ASLB) issues initial authorization of construction permits.	December 14, 1972
AEC issues construction permits.	December 15, 1972
Authorization to resume plant design engineering and construction.	January 29, 1973
Exceptions to initial construction permits filed by Mapleton and Saginaw Intervenors.	January, 1973
Atomic Safety and Licensing Appeal Board (ASLAB) affirms construction permits issued by the ASLB.	May 18, 1973
Construction of plant resumes.	June 15, 1973
Mapleton and Saginaw Intervenors petition US Court of Appeals for review of Midland construction permits.	July/August, 1973
AEC orders Consumers Power to show cause why construction should not be suspended pending a showing that the company is in full compliance with AEC quality assurance regulations.	December 3, 1973
Show cause hearing starts in Midland.	July 16, 1974

ASLB issues findings from its show cause hearing.	September 25, 1974
In–service dates of the two units delayed by one year each, to 1980 and 1981, respectively, because of utility's financial problems.	November 6, 1974
Oral argument in U.S. Court of Appeals for the D.C. Circuit on petition by Saginaw and Mapleton Intervenors to reopen construction permit hearing.	November 27, 1974
Expected dates of the operation of the two units delayed by one year each, to 1981 and 1982, respectively, because of utility's financial problems.	December 4, 1974
ASLAB affirms the initial ASLB decision on the show cause hearing.	July 30, 1975
The Michigan Court of Appeals rules against the Mapleton Intervenors' suit regarding the Midland plant.	December 9, 1975
U.S. Court of Appeals for the D.C. Circuit remands to the Nuclear Regulatory Commission for reconsideration several issues regarding the Midland construction permit.	July 21, 1976
U.S. Supreme Court grants Consumers Power Company's petition for writ of *certiorari*.	February 22, 1977
ASLB rules that construction may continue pending the resolution of the lawsuit.	September 30, 1977
Oral argument in the U.S. Supreme Court regarding the appeal of the U.S. Court of Appeals decision.	November 28, 1977
ASLAB in antitrust ruling orders Consumers Power to sell a portion of the Midland plant to other utilities.	December 30, 1977
U.S. Supreme Court overturns Court of Appeals ruling but remands radioactive waste disposal rule to the Commission and the lower court.	April 3, 1978

Source: Adapted from "Important Progress Dates: Midland Nuclear Plant," Consumers Power Company, Jackson, Michigan.

Appendix B
Table of Cases

Aberdeen and Rockfish Railroad Co. v. SCRAP, 422 U.S. 289 (1975).

Alyeska Pipeline Service Co. v. Wilderness Society, 421 U.S. 240 (1975).

BPI v. AEC, 502 F.2d 424 (D.C. Cir. 1974).

Calvert Cliffs Coordinating Committee v. AEC, 449 F.2d 1109 (D.C. Cir. 1971).

Carolina Environmental Study Group v. U.S., 510 F.2d 796 (D.C. Cir. 1975).

Citizens for a Safe Environment v. AEC, 489 F.2d 1018 (3d Cir. 1973).

Citizens for Safe Power, Inc. v. NRC, 524 F.2d 1291 (D.C. Cir. 1975).

Colorado Public Interest Group v. Train, 421 U.S. 998 (1976).

Consumers Power Company v. Aeschliman, 435 U.S. 519 (1978); 98 S. Ct. 1197 (1978).

Crowther v. Seaborg, 312 F. Supp. 1205 (D. Colo. 1970).

Duke Power Co. v. Carolina Environmental Study Group, 438 U.S. 59 (1978).

Environmental Defense Fund v. Hardin, 428 F.2d 1093 (D.C. Cir. 1970).

Environmental Defense Fund v. Ruckelshaus, 439 F.2d 584 (D.C. Cir. 1971).

Ethyl Corp. v. EPA, 541 F.2d 1 (D.C. Cir.) (en banc).

Federal Communications Commission v. Pottsville Broadcasting Company, 309 U.S. 134 (1940).

FCC v. Schreiber, 381 U.S. 279 (1965).

International Harvester Co. v. Ruckelshaus, 478 F.2d 615 (D.C. Cir. 1973).

Kleppe v. Sierra Club, 427 U.S. 390 (1976).

Lloyd Harbor Study Group v. Seaborg, 1 ELT 20188 (E.D.N.Y. 1971).

Marshall v. Consumers Power Co., 237 N.W. 2d 266 (1975).

Nader v. NRC, 513 F.2d 1045 (D.C. Cir. 1975).

Nader v. Ray, 363 F. Supp. 946 (D.D.C. 1973).

Natural Resources Defense Council v. Morton, 458 F.2d 827 (D.C. Cir. 1972).

Natural Resources Defense Council v. United States Nuclear Regulatory Commission, 547 F.2d 633 (D.C. Cir. 1976).

Natural Resources Defense Council v. United States Nuclear Regulatory Commission, 582 F.2d 166 (2d. Cir. 1978).

Nelson Aeschliman v. United States Nuclear Regulatory Commission, 547 F.2d 622 (D.C. Cir. 1976).

New England Coalition on Nuclear Pollution v. United States Nuclear Regulatory Commission, 582 F.2d 87 (1978).

New Hampshire v. AEC, 395 U.S. 962 (1969).

North Anna Environmental Coalition v. USNRC, 533 F.2d 655 (D.C. Cir. 1976).

Northern States Power Co. v. State of Minnesota, 405 U.S. 1035 (1972).

Office of Communications of the United Church of Christ v. FCC, 359 F.2d 994 (D.C. Cir. 1966).

Porter County Chapter of the Izaak Walton League v. AEC, U.S. 945 (1976).

Power Reactor Development Co. v. International Union of Electric, Radio and Machine Workers, 367 U.S. 396 (1961).

Saginaw Valley Nuclear Study Group v. United States Nuclear Regulatory Commission, 547 F.2d 622 (D.C. Cir. 1976).

Scenic Hudson Preservation Conference v. FPC, 354 F.2d 608 (2d Cir. 1965); 453 F.2d 463 (2d Cir. 1971).

Scientists' Institute for Public Information, Inc. v. AEC, 481 F.2d 1079 (D.C. Cir. 1973).

Siegel v. AEC, 400 F.2d 778 (D.C. Cir. 1968).

Sierra Club v. Morton, 405 U.S. 727 (1972).

State of New Jersey, Department of Environmental Protection v. Jersey Central Power and Light Co., 351 A.2d 337 (1976).

Thermal Ecology Must Be Preserved v. AEC, 433 F.2d 524 (D.C. Cir. 1970).

UCS v. AEC, 499 F.2d 1069 (D.C. Cir. 1974).

U.S. v. Students Challenging Regulatory Agency Procedures (SCRAP), 412 U.S. 669 (1973).

Vermont Yankee Nuclear Power Corporation v. Natural Resources Defense Council, Inc. and Consumers Power Company v. Aeschliman, 435 U.S. 519 (1978); 98 S. Ct. 1197 (1978).

York Committee for a Safe Environment v. NRC, 527 F.2d 812 (D.C. Cir. 1975).

Notes

Introduction

1. Roger Smith, "The Next Three Years Look Terrible for Nuclear Power," *Nucleonics Week* 18 (24 November 1977):1.

2. *Nucleonics Week* 18 (5 May 1977):16.

3. *Nucleonics Week* 18 (6 October 1977):11.

4. *Nucleonics Week* 18 (15 December 1977):10.

5. Atomic Industrial Forum, "Profile of U.S. Nuclear Power Development," 31 December 1978, pp. 2-3.

6. The 1977 order for the two-unit Palo Verde plant in Arizona was later cancelled, and two other units put on the order books in 1977 in New York State have such indefinite timetables that they are not considered to be serious orders.

7. Justice Felix Frankfurter, quoted by Clement Vose, *Caucasians Only: The Supreme Court, the NAACP, and the Restrictive Covenant Cases* (Berkeley: University of California Press, 1959), prologue.

8. Arthur Bentley, *The Process of Government* (Chicago: University of Chicago Press, 1908).

9. David Truman, *The Governmental Process* (New York: Alfred Knopf, 1960).

10. Raymond Bauer, Ithiel de Sola Pool, and Lewis Anthony Dexter, *American Business and Public Policy* (New York: Atherton, 1963).

11. E.E. Schattschneider, *Politics, Pressures and the Tariff* (New York: Prentice-Hall, 1935).

12. Stephen K. Bailey, *Congress Makes a Law* (New York: Columbia University Press, 1950).

13. Jeffrey M. Berry, *Lobbying for the People* (Princeton, New Jersey: Princeton University Press, 1977).

14. David Vogel, "Promoting Pluralism: The Public Interest Movement and the American Reform Tradition," paper delivered at the annual meeting of the American Political Science Association, New York, New York, September, 1978.

15. Karen Orren, "Standing to Sue: Interest Group Conflict in the Federal Courts," *American Political Science Review* 70 (September, 1976): 723-741.

16. Jack Peltason, *Federal Courts in the Political Process* (New York: Random House, 1955).

17. Joseph L. Sax, *Defending the Environment* (New York: Alfred Knopf, 1971).

18. Clement Vose, "Litigation As a Form of Pressure Group Activ-

ity," *Annals of the American Academy of Political and Social Science* 319 (September, 1958): 20–31.

19. Clement Vose, *Caucasians Only: The Supreme Court, the NAACP, and the Restrictive Covenant Cases* (Berkeley: University of California Press, 1959).

20. See, for instance, Stephen L. Wasby, *The Impact of the United States Supreme Court* (Homewood, Illinois: The Dorsey Press, 1970).

21. Nelson Aeschliman et al. v. United States Nuclear Regulatory Commission and Saginaw Valley Nuclear Study Group et al. v. United States Nuclear Regulatory Commission, 547 F.2d 622 (D.C. Cir. 1976).

22. Consumers Power Company v. Aeschliman, 435 US 519 (1978); 98 S. Ct. 1197 (1978).

Chapter 1
The Economic and Political Background

1. Edison Electric Institute, *Edison Electric Institute Statistical Yearbook of the Electric Utility Industry for 1977* (New York: Edison Electric Institute, October, 1978), p. 18. The yearly growth rate of electric generation, in percent, has been calculated as follows, using the kilowatt hours generated in 1973 and 1974 for the example:

$$\frac{(\text{kilowatt hours in 1974} - \text{kilowatt hours in 1973})}{\text{kilowatt hours in 1973}} \times 100 =$$

percent growth rate from 1973 to 1974.

2. Ibid., p. 18.

3. Ibid., p. 18. It should be noted that the electricity generation growth rate rose 6.26 percent from 1975 to 1976 but again declined to 4.72 percent from 1976 to 1977. 1978 was not expected to show any additional rise in the percentage of increase in electricity generation.

4. President Jimmy Carter, "Nuclear Energy and World Order," address at the United Nations, 13 May 1976.

5. Edward Cowan, "Schlesinger Urges Conserving Energy," *The New York Times,* 24 December 1976, p. A11.

6. *Nucleonics Week,* (10 May 1979):10.

7. Ralph Nader and John Abbotts, *The Menace of Atomic Energy* (New York: W.W. Norton, 1977), p. 273.

8. Ibid., p. 276.

9. Edison Electric Institute (1978 Public Information Research Program), *The Electric Utility Industry Today* (New York: Edison Electric Institute, 1978), p. 58.

Chapter 2
The Interest Groups: Organizations and Resources

1. David Truman, *The Governmental Process* (New York: Alfred Knopf, 1960), pp. 506–507.

2. Sheldon Novick, *The Electric War: The Fight Over Nuclear Power* (San Francisco: Sierra Club Books, 1976), p. 1.

3. Jeffrey M. Berry, *Lobbying for the People* (Princeton, New Jersey: Princeton University Press, 1977), p. 7.

4. Ibid., p. 42.

5. Peter Schuck, "Public Interest Groups and the Policy Process," *Public Administration Review* 37 (March/April), 1977): 133.

6. Irvin C. Bupp and Jean-Claude Derian, *Light Water: How the Nuclear Dream Dissolved* (New York: Basic Books, 1978), p. 119.

7. Ibid., p. 121.

8. Ibid., p. 121.

9. E.F. Schumacher, *Small Is Beautiful* (New York: Harper and Row, 1975).

10. Ralph Nader and John Abbotts, *The Menace of Atomic Energy* (New York: W.W. Norton, 1977), p. 13.

11. David Horton Smith and Burt R. Baldwin, "Voluntary Associations and Volunteering in the United States," in David Horton Smith, ed., *Voluntary Action Research* (Lexington, Mass.: Lexington Books, D.C. Heath and Company, Copyright 1974, D.C. Heath and Company), p. 286. Cited in Berry, p. 287.

12. Kurt H. Hohenemser, Roger Kasperson, and Robert Kates, "The Distrust of Nuclear Power," *Science* 196 (April 1, 1977):27.

13. Nader and Abbotts, *The Menace of Atomic Energy,* pp. 59, 107.

14. Berry, *Lobbying for the People,* p. 35.

15. William Tucker, "Environmentalism and the Leisure Class," *Harper's* 225 (December, 1977):49–80.

16. Bernard Cohen, "Political Communication on the Japanese Peace Settlement," in Betty H. Zisk, ed., *American Political Interest Groups: Readings in Theory and Research* (Belmont, California: Wadsworth Publishing Co., 1969), pp. 228–29.

17. Berry, *Lobbying for the People,* pp. 60–61.

18. Georgette Jasen, "In the Fight Over Nuclear Energy's Role, Friends and Foes Are Deeply Committed," *Wall Street Journal,* 21 July 1977, p. 26.

19. Berry, *Lobbying for the People,* p. 64.

20. Ibid., pp. 186–211.

21. Novick, *The Electric War: The Fight Over Nuclear Power,* pp. 316–317.

22. Berry, *Lobbying for the People,* p. 245.

23. Ibid., p. 254.

24. "A Siege at Seabrook," *The Free Paper* (Boston, Massachusetts), 14 May, 1977, p. 1.

25. *Atomic Industrial Forum,* "The California Initiative," 9 June 1976, p. 4.

26. Schuck, "Public Interest Groups and the Policy Process," p. 134.

27. Leonard J. Theberge (President, National Legal Center for the Public Interest), address before the Atomic Industrial Forum, 23 February 1978.

28. Berry, *Lobbying for the People,* pp. 71–72.

29. Vogel, "Promoting Pluralism: The Public Interest Movement and the American Reform Tradition", paper delivered at the annual meeting of the American Political Science Association, New York, New York, September, 1978. p. 2.

30. Edward Berlin, Anthony Roisman, and Gladys Kessler, "Public Interest Law," *George Washington Law Review* 38 (May, 1970):680.

31. John Emschwiller, "Nuclear Nemesis: Using the Law's Delay, Myron Cherry Attacks Atomic Power Projects," *Wall Street Journal,* 10 March 1978, p. 1.

32. "EPRI Finds Nuclear Cheaper on Average," *Nuclear News* 20 (December, 1977):35.

33. Atomic Industrial Forum, "1978 Economic Survey Results," 14 May 1979, p. 4 (Table of "U.S. Electrical Generating Costs and Power Plant Performance in 1978").

34. Jack Anderson, "Nuclear Industry Blasts TV Networks," *Detroit Free Press,* 26 June 1977, p. 3C.

35. For a full discussion of the Westinghouse Electric Corporation's political activities, see its publication *Resources: Nuclear Energy Information.*

36. Nader and Abbotts, *The Menace of Atomic Energy,* p. 226.

37. Consumers Power Company, *Inside* 16 December 1977, p. 1.

38. Atomic Industrial Forum, "Profile of U.S. Nuclear Power Development," 31 December 1978, pp. 2–3.

39. Although the price of uranium rose significantly, the cost of its mining and milling represents only a fraction of the total fuel cost which, in turn, is only a small fraction of the expense involved in a nuclear plant.

40. Obviously, some of the postponements one year became cancellations another year, as cited by Don S. Smith and A. Angela Lancaster, "Nuclear Power's Effects on Electric Rate Making," *Public Utilities Fortnightly* 101 (2 February 1978):21.

41. Jasen, "In the Fight Over Nuclear Energy's Role, Friends and Foes Are Deeply Committed," p. 26.

42. As mentioned in chapter 1, there were four nuclear reactors actu-

ally ordered in 1977. However, two of them (the two–unit Palo Verde plant in Arizona) have been cancelled, and the other two in New York State have such an indefinite timetable that they are not considered to be serious orders.

43. David Burnham, "G.E. Warns of Halt in Making Reactors," *The New York Times,* 15 May 1977, p. 1.

44. Nader and Abbotts, *The Menace of Atomic Energy,* p. 265, citing United States Atomic Energy Commission, WASH–1174, *The Nuclear Industry 1974* (Washington, D.C., 1975), p. 1.

45. Atomic Industrial Forum, *INFO* (January, 1978), p. 7.

46. Atomic Industrial Forum, "1978 Economic Survey Results," 14 May 1979, p. 4 (table of "U.S. Electrical Generating Costs and Power Plant Performance in 1978").

47. Jasen, "In the Fight Over Nuclear Energy's Role, Friends and Foes Are Deeply Committed," p. 26.

48. Gladwyn Hill, "California's Case Study in Nuclear Politics," *The New York Times,* 5 March 1978, p. E3.

49. Robert Georgine (AFL–CIO), address before the Edison Electric Institute, 45th Annual Convention, 14 June 1977.

50. "Labor Would Accelerate Use of Coal, Nuclear," *Nuclear News* 20 (April, 1977):54.

51. "Three Thousand Pronuclears Hold Manchester Rally," *Nuclear News* (20 August, 1977):50.

52. Bayard Rustin (A. Philip Randolph Institute), address before the Edison Electric Institute, 45th Annual Convention, 14 June 1977.

53. John E. Peterson, "Energy Plan Dooms Poor, NAACP Says," *Detroit News,* 8 January 1978, p. 1.

54. Ibid., p. 1.

Chapter 3
The Role of the Nuclear Regulatory Commission

1. Quoted by Archibald Cox, *The Role of the Supreme Court in American Government* (New York: Oxford University Press, 1976), p. 1.

2. Arthur W. Murphy, *The Nuclear Power Controversy* (Englewood Cliffs, New Jersey: Prentice-Hall, 1976), p. 113.

3. Arthur W. Murphy, "The National Environmental Policy Act and the Licensing Process: Environmentalist Magna Carta or Agency Coup de Grace," *Columbia Law Review* 72 (October, 1972):994.

4. Steve Ebbin and Raphael Kasper, *Citizen Groups and the Nuclear Power Controversy* (Cambridge, Massachusetts: The MIT Press, 1974), p. 172.

5. Ibid., pp. 174–5.

6. See Kenneth C. Davis, *Administrative Law Text,* Third Edition (St. Paul, Minnesota: West Publishing Co., 1972), pp. 574–78.

7. Joseph L. Sax, *Defending the Environment* (New York: Alfred Knopf, 1971), pp. 125–136.

8. Nader v. NRC, 513 F.2d 1045 (D.C. Cir. 1975), 1045.

9. Lloyd Harbor Study Group v. Seaborg, 1 ELR 20188 (E.D.N.Y. 1971) and Thermal Ecology Must Be Preserved v. AEC, 433 F.2d 524 (D.C. Cir. 1970).

10. Karen Orren, "Standing to Sue: Interest Group Conflict in the Federal Courts," *American Political Science Review,* 70 (September, 1976): 726.

11. David Truman, *The Governmental Process* (New York: Alfred Knopf, 1960), p. 488.

12. David Vogel, "Promoting Pluralism: The Public Interest Movement and the American Reform Tradition," paper delivered at the annual meeting of the American Political Science Association, New York, New York, September, 1978.

13. Sax, *Defending the Environment,* p. xxii. It should be noted, however, that the judiciary has protected the interests of the individual and the minority group more assiduously during some historical periods than others.

14. Berry, *Lobbying for the People,* p. 56.

15. Interview with Mary Sinclair, leader of the Saginaw Valley Nuclear Study Group, Ann Arbor, Michigan, 11 October 1978.

16. Nader and Abbotts, *The Menace of Atomic Energy* (New York: W.W. Norton, 1977), p. 277, citing Common Cause, "Serving Two Masters," (Washington, D.C.: October, 1976), pp. 24–27.

17. Ibid., p. 278.

18. Frank Graham, Jr., "The Outrageous Mr. Cherry and the Underachieving Nukes," *Audubon* 79 (September, 1977):57, quoting Myron Cherry.

19. Roger Smith, "Stabilizing Nuclear Licensing Requirements Essential, Says AIF Report," *Nucleonics Week* 19 (26 January 1978):1.

Chapter 4
The Role of the Judiciary in Nuclear Power Cases

1. Warren Weaver, Jr., "Inevitably, the Environment Has Gone to Court," *The New York Times,* 30 October 1977, p. E2.

2. Karen Orren, "Standing to Sue: Interest Group Conflict in the Federal Courts," *American Political Science Review* 70 (September, 1976): 723.

3. 354 F.2d 608 (2d Cir. 1965).

4. Orren, "Standing to Sue: Interest Group Conflict in the Federal Courts," p. 733.

5. 359 F.2d 994 (D.C. Cir. 1966).

6. 428 F.2d 1093 (D.C. Cir. 1970), 1097.

7. Orren, "Standing to Sue: Interest Group Conflict in the Federal Courts," p. 737.

8. 405 U.S. 727 (1972).

9. 412 U.S. 669 (1973).

10. See Louis L. Jaffe, "Standing Again," *Harvard Law Review* 84 (January, 1971):633–38; Kenneth Scott, "Standing in the Supreme Court," *Harvard Law Review* 86 (February, 1973):645–92; Robert A. Sedler, "Standing Justiciability, and All That," *Vanderbilt Law Review* 25 (April, 1972):479–512; Lee A. Albert, "Standing to Challenge Administrative Action," *Yale Law Journal* 83 (January, 1974):425–97.

11. Scott, p. 692.

12. 502 F.2d 424 (D.C. Cir. 1974).

13. 489 F.2d 1018 (3d Cir. 1973).

14. 421 U.S. 240 (1975).

15. 367 U.S. 396 (1961).

16. 280 F.2d 645 (D.C. Cir. 1960).

17. 367 U.S. 396 (1961), 408.

18. Ibid., 409.

19. Martin Shapiro, *The Supreme Court and Administrative Agencies* (New York: Free Press, 1968), p. 264.

20. Ibid., p. 269.

21. The Atomic Energy Commission in 1971, on the initiative of its own task force, conducted a series of tests of the emergency core cooling system (ECCS) of nuclear reactors, which is the safety system designed to operate in the event of a loss of coolant from a pressurized water reactor. The experiments showed results that differed from the computer simulations on which the AEC had been basing its safety requirements, so the agency revised its ECCS design standards. Because the original standards had been demonstrably unjustified by the model test standards, the new standards were also disputed as untenable by intervenors in the public Rule-Making Hearing that extended over an eighteen–month period. It resulted in further AEC revisions and new ECCS "acceptance criteria." The importance of the ECCS controversy is that it stimulated intervenor questioning of the "overall social acceptability of reactors." Bupp and Derian, p. 134.

22. 363 F. Supp. 946 (D.D.C. 1973).

23. 499 F.2d 1069 (D.C. Cir. 1974).

24. 513 F.2d 1045 (D.C. Cir. 1975).

25. 367 U.S. 396 (1961).

26. 423 U.S. 12 (1975); 429 U.S. 945 (1976).

27. 533 F.2d 655 (D.C. Cir. 1976).

28. 312 F. Supp. 1205 (D. Colo. 1970).

29. 527 F.2d 812 (D.C. Cir. 1975).

30. 405 U.S. 1035 (1972).

31. Ibid., 1154.

32. 351 A.2d 337 (1976).

33. Arthur W. Murphy and D. Bruce La Pierre, "Nuclear 'Moratorium' Legislation in the States and the Supremacy Clause: A Case of Express Preemption," *Columbia Law Review* 76(April, 1976):456.

34. "Slaying the Nuclear Giants: Is California's New Nuclear Power Plant Siting Legislation Shielded Against the Attack of Federal Preemption?" *Pacific Law Journal* 8 (July, 1977):781.

35. 400 F.2d 778 (D.C. Cir. 1968).

36. Lee Bohn Fawkes, "Environmental Law—Nuclear Power Plants," *Annual Survey of American Law* (1976), p. 588.

37. 421 U.S. 998 (1976).

38. Kenneth C. Davis, *Administrative Law,* Sixth Edition (St. Paul, Minnesota: West Publishing, 1977), p. 590.

39. Murphy, "The National Environmental Policy Act and the Licensing Process," p. 966.

40. 395 U.S. 962 (1969). This ruling generated Congressional concern about thermal pollution. Consequently, Senator Edmund Muskie's Water Quality Improvement Act of 1970 was intended to apply to power plants. It required that evidence of compliance with state water quality standards be acquired prior to the issuance of a federal license for the conduct of activities resulting in discharges into navigable waters.

41. 449 F.2d 1109 (D.C. Cir. 1971).

42. Ibid., 1123.

43. Murphy, "The National Environmental Policy Act and the Licensing Process," p. 969.

44. Orren, "Standing to Sue: Interest Group Conflict in the Federal Courts," p. 740.

45. Richard A. Liroff, *A National Policy for the Environment: NEPA and Its Aftermath* (Bloomington, Indiana: Indiana University Press, 1976), p. 129.

46. 481 F.2d 1079 (D.C. Cir. 1973).

47. 312 F. Supp. 1205 (D. Colo. 1970).

48. 524 F.2d 1291 (D.C. Cir. 1975).

49. The Commission has classified nine levels of hypothetical nuclear reactor accidents, with Class 1 being a trivial accident with a high probability of occurrence, and Class 9 being a catastrophic accident with extreme unlikelihood of occurrence. A Class 9 accident would occur if, for instance,

the reactor's primary cooling system were to fail causing a loss-of-coolant accident, followed by a simultaneous failure in the back-up system, the ECCS. According to the Commission, the probability of this occurrence is one chance in ten million or more for the operation of one nuclear plant in a one-year period. Brief for the AEC, Nelson Aeschliman v. United States Atomic Energy Commission, 547 F.2d 622 (D.C. Cir. 1976).

50. 510 F.2d 796 (D.C. Cir. 1975).

51. Ibid., 801.

52. Ibid., 801.

53. Fawkes, "Environmental Law—Nuclear Power Plants," p. 608.

54. Jack Peltason, *Federal Courts in the Political Process* (New York: Random House, 1955), p. 11.

55. 405 U.S. 1035 (1972).

56. Even though the court had ruled that the utility did not have to comply with the strict state standards for radioactive emissions and could build its plant to the Commission's more liberal standards, the utility decided to comply with the state anyway. This decision cost the utility an extra $17 million in new equipment. Interview with Roland Jensen, Director of Corporate Strategic Planning, Northern States Power Company, Minneapolis, Minnesota, 14 May 1978.

57. 449 F.2d 1109 (D.C. Cir. 1971).

58. "Dow Seeks Early N-Hearing," *Midland Daily News,* 2 August 1971, p. 1.

59. John Emschwiller, "Nuclear Nemesis: Using the Law's Delay, Myron Cherry Attacks Atomic Power Projects," *The Wall Street Journal* 10 March 1978, p. 1.

60. Daniel Fiorino, "The Federal Courts and the Regulatory Process: The Cases of Natural Gas and Broadcasting," (Ph.D. diss., Johns Hopkins University, 1977), p. 337.

61. "Rushing for Judgments," editorial, *The New York Times,* 23 July 1978, p. 18E.

62. Richard A. Liroff, *A National Policy for the Environment: NEPA and its Aftermath* (Bloomington, Indiana: Indiana University Press, 1976), p. 155.

63. "Rushing for Judgments," p. 18E.

64. 405 U.S. 1035 (1972).

65. 429 U.S. 945 (1976).

66. Irvin C. Bupp and Jean-Claude Derian, *Light Water: How the Nuclear Dream Dissolved* (New York: Basic Books, 1978), p. 157.

67. "Washington and the Utilities," *Public Utilities Fortnightly* 101 (April 13, 1978):35.

68. Frances Gendlin, "The Palisades Protest: A Pattern of Citizen Intervention," *Science and Public Affairs* 27 (November, 1971):53.

69. William Thomas Keating, "Politics, Energy and the Environment," *American Behavioral Scientist* 19 (September/October, 1975):61.

Chapter 5
The Interest Groups at Midland

1. Interview with Mary Sinclair, leader of the Saginaw Valley Nuclear Study Group, Ann Arbor, Michigan, 11 October 1978.

2. *Petition for Leave to Intervene,* (Citizens Committee for the Environmental Protection of Michigan) 12 November 1970, p. 3, quoted in Steve Ebbin and Raphael Kasper, *Citizen Groups and the Nuclear Power Controversy* (Cambridge, Massachusetts: The MIT Press, 1974), p. 64.

3. Ebbin and Kasper, *Citizen Groups and the Nuclear Power Controversy,* p. 189.

4. Gay McGee, "Midland Housewife Initiated Nuclear Plant Hassle," *Bay City Times,* 6 June 1971, p. C1.

5. Interview with Mary Sinclair, 11 October 1978.

6. Peter Steketee, Chairman of the West Michigan Environmental Action Council, "Letter to the Editor," *Midland Daily News,* 26 April 1971, p. 4.

7. Kenneth Rathje, Chairman of the Saginaw UAW Community Action Program Council, "Letter to the Editor," *Midland Daily News,* 20 August 1971, p. 4.

8. Telephone interview with Dr. Daniel Luria, UAW Research Department, Detroit, Michigan, 18 October 1978.

9. John O'Connor, "High Court Hearing Is Expensive," *Jackson Citizen Patriot,* 29 May 1978, p. 4.

10. *Petition for Leave to Intervene,* (University of Michigan Environmental Law Society) 12 November 1970, p. 8, quoted in Ebbin and Kasper, p. 65.

11. "N–Hearing Zeroes in on Birds, Fish and Trees," *Bay City Times,* 30 May 1972, p. 3A.

12. *Petition for Leave to Intervene,* (State of Kansas), quoted in "Kansas Likely to Enter Midland N–Plant Case," *Midland Daily News,* 18 September 1971, p. 1.

13. Among these organizations were the Michigan Steelhead and Salmon Association; the Michigan Lakes and Streams Association; the Minnesota Environmental Control Citizens Association; and Lloyd Harbor Study Group of Long Island, New York; the Grand Mere Association of Stevensville, Michigan; Environment, Inc., of Whitehall, Michigan; the Bowling Green State Students' Environmental Association of Bowling Green, Ohio; Guard of San Clemente, California; and the Oregon Environmental Coali-

tion of Portland, Oregon. These organizations planned to make limited appearances at the licensing hearings, according to an article written by Mary Sinclair, "Historic Case Will Test AEC Powers, Standards and Licensing Practices," *Essexville-Hampton Observer,* 19 November 1970, p. 1.

14. Fred E. Garrett, "Attorney's Lawsuit 'a Terrible Tangle'," *Saginaw News,* 25 January 1978, p. B4.

15. Interview with Mary Sinclair, 11 October 1978.

16. John Emschwiller, "Nuclear Nemesis: Using the Law's Delay, Myron Cherry Attacks Atomic Power Projects," *The Wall Street Journal,* 10 March 1978, p. 1. Reprinted with permission.

17. Frank Graham, Jr., "The Outrageous Mr. Cherry and the Underachieving Nukes," *Audubon* 79 (September, 1977):57.

18. Emschwiller, "Nuclear Nemesis: Using the Law's Delay, Myron Cherry Attacks Atomic Power Projects," p. 1. Reprinted with permission.

19. Nader and Abbotts, *The Menace of Atomic Energy* (New York: W.W. Norton, 1977), p. 329.

20. "Dow Hits Tactics of Nuclear Foes," *Midland Daily News,* 18 January 1971, p. 1.

21. Irving Like, "Multi-Media Confrontation—The Environmentalists' Strategy for a 'No-Win' Agency Proceeding," *Atomic Energy Law Journal* 13 (Spring, 1971):1.

22. Ebbin and Kasper, *Citizen Groups and the Nuclear Power Controversy,* p. 148.

23. Phillip L. Schneider, "Motion to Dismiss Mapleton Intervenors on Tap Monday," *Midland Daily News,* 20 May 1972, p. 1.

24. William P. Golden, "Wives Will Rejoice in Midland A-Plant," *Jackson Citizen Patriot,* 17 December 1967, p. 1.

25. Betty Herring, "McConnell Says No Need for Fear Over N-Plant," *Midland Daily News,* 22 October 1970, p. 1.

26. "Firm Will Cut Radioactive Waste at Plant," *Midland Daily News,* 29 March 1971, p. 1.

27. Graham, "The Outrageous Mr. Cherry and the Underachieving Nukes," p. 57.

28. "N-Plant Construction Delayed Pending OK," *Midland Daily News,* 14 November 1970, p. 1.

29. "N-Plant Backers Refute Claims by Mrs. Sinclair," *Midland Daily News,* 23 August 1971, p. 1.

30. "N-Plant Endorsed by Five Labor Unions," *Midland Daily News,* 5 October 1971, p. 1.

31. Among these organizations were the Midland Nature Club, the Midland area realtors, the Midland section of the American Institute of Chemical Engineers, the Midland County Cancer Society, the Michigan

AFL–CIO, District 29 of the United Steel Workers of America, the Michigan Conference of Teamsters, and the Midland Jaycees.

32. "Shutdown of Midland Sought During Rally for Nuclear Plant," *Midland Daily News,* 30 September 1971, p. 1.

33. "In Nuclear–Powered Bind," editorial, *Bay City Times,* 7 December 1969, p. 4.

34. "Small Step Forward in Power Controversy," editorial, *Midland Daily News,* 18 March 1971, p. 4.

35. "Final Questions Must End 'N' Plant Delay," editorial, *Midland Daily News,* 13 April 1971, p. 4.

36. Graham, "The Outrageous Mr. Cherry and the Underachieving Nukes," p. 63.

37. Arthur W. Murphy, "The National Environmental Policy Act and the Licensing Process: Environmentalist Magna Carta or Agency Coup de Grace," *Columbia Law Review* 72 (October, 1972):963–1007.

38. Exceptions of the Intervenors before the Atomic Safety and Licensing Appeal Board, 15 January 1973, p. 142.

39. "Chronology of Project Cost Revisions," Consumers Power Company, Jackson, Michigan, 1976.

Chapter 6
The Midland Case in the U.S. Court of Appeals

1. Interview with Mary Sinclair, 11 October 1978.

2. Ibid.

3. John Emschwiller, "Nuclear Nemesis: Using the Law's Delay, Myron Cherry Attacks Atomic Power Projects," *The Wall Street Journal,* 10 March 1978, p. 1. Reprinted with permission.

4. 237 N.W. 2d 266 (1975).

5. Interview with Leonard J. Theberge, President, National Legal Center for the Public Interest, Washington, D.C., 17 May 1978.

6. Interview with Judd Bacon, Managing Attorney, Consumers Power Company, Jackson, Michigan, 19 September 1978.

7. 547 F.2d 622 (D.C. Cir. 1976).

8. 547 F.2d 633 (D.C. Cir. 1976).

9. The issues that were dismissed included quality assurance requirements, emergency core cooling system (ECCS) standards, fogging and icing problems, and class nine accidents. Nelson Aeschliman et al. v. United States Nuclear Regulatory Commission, 547 F.2d 622 (D.C. Cir. 1976), 632.

10. The waste disposal issue refers to the storage of radioactive waste products (resulting from nuclear fission in light water reactors) until they slowly detoxify to the point that they are no longer hazardous. A synony-

mous term is fuel cycle issue which also refers to this last stage of the chain of activities involving the use of uranium in nuclear reactors.

11. Aeschliman, p. 630, quoting ACRS Report to the AEC, Midland Reactors, June 18, 1970, pp. 5-6.

12. Brief for the petitioners, Aeschliman, p. 16.

13. Brief for the respondents, Aeschliman, p. 28.

14. Aeschliman, p. 631.

15. Ibid., p. 631.

16. Ibid., p. 631.

17. Brief for petitioners, Aeschliman, p. 37.

18. Aeschliman, p. 625, citing Natural Resources Defense Council v. Morton, 458 F.2d 827 (D.C. Cir. 1972).

19. Aeschliman, p. 625, quoting the ASLB opinion.

20. Brief for the respondents, Aeschliman, p. 43.

21. Aeschliman, p. 627, citing 449 F.2d 1109 (D.C. Cir. 1971), 1118.

22. Ibid., p. 627.

23. Aeschliman, p. 628-29.

24. Ibid., p. 632.

25. Ibid., p. 632.

26. 547 F.2d 633 (D.C. Cir. 1976).

27. Interviews with Judd Bacon, September 19, 1978, and Mary Sinclair, 11 October 1978.

28. Brief for petitioners, Aeschliman, p. 49.

29. Natural Resources Defense Council v. United States Nuclear Regulatory Commission, 547 F.2d 633, p. 653 (D.C. Cir. 1976).

30. Ibid., p. 633.

31. Ibid., p. 644-646.

32. Ibid., p. 656.

33. Ibid., p. 660.

34. Ibid., p. 641.

35. See especially Clement Vose, *Caucasians Only: The Supreme Court, the NAACP, and the Restrictive Covenant Cases* (Berkeley: University of California Press, 1959).

36. Richard Liroff, *A National Policy for the Environment: NEPA and Its Aftermath* (Bloomington, Indiana: Indiana University Press, 1976), pp. 156-157.

37. Ibid., pp. 156-157.

38. 449 F.2d 1109 (D.C. Cir. 1971).

39. 513 F.2d 1045 (D.C. Cir. 1975).

40. 527 F.2d 812 (D.C. Cir. 1975).

41. 524 F.2d 1291 (D.C. Cir. 1975).

42. 510 F.2d 796 (D.C. Cir. 1975).

43. Warren Gardner and I. Michael Greensberger, "Judicial Review of

Administrative Action and Responsible Government," *Georgetown Law Journal* 63 (October, 1974):7–38.

44. 439 F.2d 584 (D.C. Cir. 1971).

45. 478 F.2d 615, 652 (D.C. Cir. 1973).

46. 541 F.2d 1, 67 (D.C. Cir.) (en banc).

47. NRDC v. NRC, 652.

48. Glendon Schubert, *Judicial Policy-Making: The Political Role of the Courts* (Chicago: Scott, Foresman, 1965), p. 112, citing Representative Wright Patman.

49. Anthony Z. Roisman, "Suing for Safety," *Trial* 10 (January–February, 1974):13–16.

50. NRDC v. NRC, 643, citing: Stephen Williams, "'Hybrid Rule-making' under the Administrative Procedure Act," *University of Chicago Law Review* 42 (1975):401; Skelly Wright, "Court of Appeals Review of Federal Regulatory Agency Rulemaking," *Administrative Law Review* 26 (1974):199; S. Wright, "The Courts and the Rulemaking Process: The Limits of Judicial Review," *Cornell Law Review* 59 (1974):375; Paul Verkuil, "Judicial Review of Informal Rulemaking," *Virginia Law Review* 60 (1974):234–249; "The Judicial Role in Defining Procedural Requirements for Agency Rulemaking," *Harvard Law Review* 87 (1974):782; Robert Hamilton, "Procedures for the Adoption of Rules of General Applicability: The Need for Procedural Innovation in Administrative Rule-making," *California Law Review* 60 (1972):1276, 1313–30; B.M. Claggett, "Informal Action–Adjudication–Rulemaking," *Duke Law Journal* 51 (1971):78.

51. Williams, "'Hybrid Rulemaking' under the Administrative Procedure Act," p. 401.

52. NRDC v. NRC, 652, citing *Smithsonian Magazine* (April, 1974) 5:20.

53. NRDC v. NRC, 648, citing *Science* 188 (April, 25, 1975):345.

54. NRDC v. NRC. 648, citing *Science* 190 (October 24, 1975):361.

55. NRDC v. NRC, 648, citing *Washington Post,* 11 May 1976, p. A2.

56. NRDC v. NRC, 648, citing *Business Week* (February 2, 1976):17.

57. NRDC v. NRC, 648, citing *Science and Government Report* 6 (February 1, 1976):8.

58. Aeschliman, p. 629.

59. Report of the American Assembly, *Nuclear Energy* 22–25 April 1976, p. 6.

60. The first state referendum on nuclear power had been held in California in June, 1976, a month prior to the Midland ruling, with a two-to-one vote in favor of the nuclear industry.

61. NRDC v. NRC, 655.

62. Interview with Judd Bacon, 19 September 1978.

Chapter 7
The Midland Case in the Supreme Court

1. "Nuclear News Briefs," *Nuclear News* 20 (February, 1977):17.
2. Interview with Judd Bacon, 19 September 1978.
3. Atomic Industrial Forum, *INFO* 98 (September, 1976):2.
4. *Nucleonics Week* 18 (13 January 1977):9.
5. 435 U.S. 519 (1978); 98 S. Ct. 1197 (1978).
6. Warren Weaver, Jr., "Burger Court is Limiting Its Own Turf," *The New York Times,* 9 April 1978, p. 2E.
7. Vermont Yankee Nuclear Power Corporation v. Natural Resources Defense Council, Inc. and Consumers Power Company v. Aeschliman 435 U.S. 519 (1978), 557, quoting brief for Consumers Power Company, p. 37.
8. Brief for Saginaw Intervenors, p. 2.
9. Vermont Yankee, p. 539.
10. Ibid., p. 539.
11. Ibid., p. 541.
12. Aberdeen and Rockfish Railroad Co. v. SCRAP, 422 US 289, 319 (1975); United States v. SCRAP, 412 U.S. 669, 694 (1973); Kleppe v. Sierra Club, 427 U.S. 390, 405–406 (1976).
13. Vermont Yankee, p. 548.
14. Ibid., p. 525.
15. Ibid., p. 524, citing FCC v. Schreiber, 381 U.S. 279, 290 (1965); Federal Communications Commission v. Pottsville Broadcasting Co., 309 U.S. 134, 138 (1940).
16. Vermont Yankee, p. 546.
17. Ibid.
18. Ibid., p. 547.
19. Ibid., p. 558.
20. The Supreme Court here agreed with the concurring opinion in the Vermont Yankee Court of Appeals case written by Judge Tamm.
21. Vermont Yankee, p. 551.
22. Ibid., p. 551.
23. Ibid., p. 551.
24. Ibid., p. 552.
25. Ibid., p. 547.
26. Ibid., pp. 553–554.
27. Ibid., p. 555, quoting Kleppe v. Sierra Club, 47 U.S. 390, 410 (1976).
28. Vermont Yankee, footnote, p. 555.
29. Ibid., p. 556.
30. Ibid., p. 556.
31. Ibid., p. 556.

32. Ibid., p. 557.

33. Ibid., pp. 557–558.

34. Ibid., pp. 557–558.

35. Ibid., p. 525.

36. Weaver, p. 2E.

37. Vermont Yankee, p. 558.

38. Ibid., footnote, 537.

39. Kenneth C. Davis, *Administrative Law of the Seventies* (Rochester, New York: Lawyers Co-operative Publishing Company, 1976), p. 10.

40. Charles Lamb, "Exploring the Conservatism of Federal Appeals Court Judges," *Indiana Law Journal* 51 (Winter, 1976):263.

41. J.W. Howard, "Litigation Flow in Three U.S. Courts of Appeals," *Law and Society Review* 8 (Fall, 1973):43.

42. Interviews with Mary Sinclair, 11 October 1978, and Judd Bacon, 19 September 1978.

43. Interview with Judd Bacon, 19 September 1978.

44. Vermont Yankee, p. 540.

45. "Carter's Lawyer Calls Own Shots," *Detroit Free Press,* 29 December 1977, p. 1B.

46. Brief for the Federal Respondents, p. 61.

48. Robert Scigliano, *The Supreme Court and the Presidency* (New York: Free Press, 1971), pp. 177–180.

48. Robert Stern, "The Solicitor General's Office and Administrative Agency Litigation," *American Bar Association Journal* 46 (February 1960): 218.

49. Glendon Schubert, *Judicial Policy–Making: The Political Role of the Courts* (Chicago: Scott, Foresman, 1965), p. 112.

50. Norman Dupont, "Judicial Review of Generic Rulemaking," *Georgetown Law Journal* 65 (June, 1977):1312.

51. Laurel Breitkopf, "The National Environmental Policy Act of 1969 and Nuclear Power Plant Licensing," *DePaul Law Review* 26 (Spring, 1977):677.

52. "Environmental Law: Public Participation in the Environmental Impact Statement Process," *Minnesota Law Review* 61 (January, 1977): 381.

53. J. Michael McGarry, III, and Troy B. Conner, Jr., "Nuclear Alternative: An Analysis of Paralysis," *Hastings Law Journal* 28 (May, 1977):1242.

54. "Implementing the National Environmental Policy Act through Rulemaking: The Implications of NRDC v. NRC," *University of Pennsylvania Law Review* 126 (November, 1977):150.

55. David Bazelon, "The Impact of the Courts on Public Administration," *Indiana Law Journal* 52 (Fall, 1976):104.

56. David Bazelon, "Coping with Technology through the Legal Process," *Cornell Law Review* 62 (June, 1977):819.

57. Vermont Yankee, p. 547.

58. Skelly Wright, "The Courts and the Rulemaking Process: The Limits of Judical Review," *Cornell Law Review* 59 (1974):375, 387–388.

59. Brief for the Federal Respondents, pp. 45–46.

60. Archibald Cox, *The Role of the Supreme Court in American Government* (New York: Oxford University Press, 1976), p. 99.

61. Ibid., p. 103.

62. Ibid., pp. 103–104.

63. Raoul Berger, *Government by Judiciary: The Transformation of the Fourteenth Amendment* (Cambridge, Massachusetts: Harvard University Press, 1977):410.

64. Ibid., pp. 417, 410.

65. Vermont Yankee, p. 549.

66. Ibid., p. 557.

67. David Rohde and Harold Spaeth, *Supreme Court Decision Making* (San Francisco: W.H. Freeman, 1976):155.

68. Jack Anderson and Les Whitten, "Atomic Watergate Operation," syndicated column, 11 August 1977.

69. Frank Graham, Jr., "The Outrageous Mr. Cherry and the Underachieving Nukes," *Audubon* 79 (September, 1977):54–55.

70. John Emschwiller, "Nuclear Nemesis: Using the Law's Delay, Myron Cherry Attacks Atomic Power Projects," *The Wall Street Journal*, 10 March 1978, p. 1. Reprinted with permission.

71. Ibid., p. 1. Reprinted with permission.

72. John A. Puravs, "We Got More Heat Than Light," *Saginaw News*, 25 April 1978, p. A7.

73. Vermont Yankee, p. 558.

Chapter 8
The Impact of the Judicial Ruling

1. "Supreme Court Defines Narrower Role for Courts in Nuclear Field," *Nucleonics Week* 19, (6 April 1978):3.

2. 435 US 519 (1978), 558.

3. Sandra L. Dickey, "N–Plant Legal Fight Nearly Over," *Saginaw News*, 4 April 1978, p. 1.

4. Fred E. Garrett, "Suit Reflects Nuclear 'Fallout'," *Saginaw News*, 29 January 1978, p. G1.

5. Interview with Mary Sinclair, 11 October 1978.

6. Telephone interview with Judd Bacon, 8 June 1979.

7. Interview with Mary Sinclair, 11 October 1978.

8. John Emschwiller, "Nuclear Nemesis: Using the Law's Delay, Myron Cherry Attacks Atomic Power Projects," *The Wall Street Journal,* 10 March 1978, p. 1. Reprinted with permission.

9. Lynn Stevens, "NRC Attorneys Trying to Ban Myron Cherry from All Licensing Proceedings," *Nucleonics Week* 19 (5 January 1978):3.

10. *Nucleonics Week* 19 (30 March 1978):4; *Nucleonics Week* 19 (18 May 1978):9–10.

11. "Clergymen Rip Midland Nuclear Plants," *Detroit News,* 30 April 1978, p. 25B.

12. The funding was authorized by the Energy Conservation and Production Act of 1976 and the Public Utility Regulatory Policies Act of 1978. Telephone interview with Roderick S. Coy, Assistant Attorney General for the State of Michigan, Lansing, Michigan, 25 October 1979.

13. Pete Plastrik, "Nuclear Safety Spurs State Action," *Jackson Citizen Patriot,* 6 June 1978, p. 3.

14. Emschwiller, "Nuclear Nemesis: Using the Law's Delay, Myron Cherry Attacks Atomic Power Projects," p. 1. Reprinted with permission.

15. Consumers Power Company Press Release, 3 April 1978.

16. Consumers Power Company, "Chronology of Project Cost Revisions."

17. "Nuclear Plant Lag Rapped by Utility," *Jackson Citizen Patriot,* 1 November 1978, p. 1.

18. Ibid., p. 1.

19. Emschwiller, "Nuclear Nemesis: Using the Law's Delay, Myron Cherry Attacks Atomic Power Projects," p. 1. Reprinted with permission.

Chapter 9
Legal Advocacy and the Nuclear Power Controversy

1. See chapter 8 for a description of the federal funding that already exists for public interest group intervention in regulatory proceedings involving electric rates.

2. Calvert Cliffs Coordinating Committee v. AEC, 449 F.2d 1109 (D.C. Cir. 1971).

3. "Nuclear Plant Lag Rapped by Utility," *Jackson Citizen Patriot,* 1 November 1978, p. 1.

4. Roger Smith, "Utilities Would Buy Nuclear—If Only Carter Speaks Out, Industry Feels," *Nucleonics Week* 20, (29 March 1979):2–3.

5. Irving Kristol, American Enterprise Institute address, 13 June 1977.

6. The most notable example of legal advocacy by the nuclear indus-

try now is the current Westinghouse Corporation suit against the Nuclear Regulatory Commission, argued in the Third Circuit Court of Appeals in February, 1977, regarding the resumption of the GESMO (generic environmental statement on the use of mixed oxide fuel) rulemaking proceeding on plutonium recycling.

7. Interview with Leonard J. Theberge, President, National Legal Center for the Public Interest, Washington, D.C., 17 May 1978.

8. Interview with Leonard J. Theberge, 17 May 1978.

9. It should be noted, however, that Kenneth Davis, one of the leading administrative law scholars, believes that the impact of the Supreme Court's broad dictum on rulemaking procedures will only be temporary. He is very critical of the Supreme Court's comments that "the courts may not add to the procedural requirements of section 553" of the APA by expanding the nature of informal rulemaking procedures, as Bazelon had tried to do. Davis asserts that the Court's ruling was too broad for the case at hand and undermined the thrust of the court of appeals rulings of the 1970's on rulemaking procedures, as well as differing from previous Supreme Court opinions. Kenneth Culp Davis, *Administrative Law Treatise,* 2nd ed. vol. 1 (San Diego: University of California, 1978), pp. 605–616.

10. 582 F.2d 166 (2d Cir. 1978).

11. Duke Power Co. v. Carolina Environmental Study Group, 438 U.S. 59 (1978).

12. New England Coalition on Nuclear Pollution v. United States Nuclear Regulatory Commission, 582 F.2d 87 (1978).

13. Interview with Joseph Sax, Professor of Law, University of Michigan, Ann Arbor, Michigan, 3 October 1978.

14. Interview with Joseph Sax, 3 October 1978.

15. *Nucleonics Week* 19 (28 September 1978):11.

16. Interviews with Joseph Sax, Professor of Law, University of Michigan, 3 October 1978, and Mary Sinclair, leader of the Saginaw Valley Nuclear Study Group, Ann Arbor, Michigan, 11 October 1978.

17. Leonard J. Theberge, President, National Legal Center for the Public Interest, Address before the Atomic Industrial Forum, 23 February 1978, p. 10. Reprinted with permission.

Selected Bibliography

Books

Bailey, Stephen K. *Congress Makes a Law*. New York: Columbia University Press, 1950.

Bauer, Raymond; Pool, Ithiel de Sola; and Dexter, Lewis Anthony. *American Business and Public Policy*. New York: Atherton, 1963.

Bentley, Arthur. *The Process of Government*. Chicago: University of Chicago Press, 1908.

Berger, Raoul. *Government by Judiciary: The Transformation of the Fourteenth Amendment*. Cambridge, Massachusetts: Harvard University Press, 1977.

Berry, Jeffrey M. *Lobbying for the People*. Princeton, New Jersey: Princeton University Press, 1977.

Bupp, Irvin C. and Derian, Jean-Claude. *Light Water: How the Nuclear Dream Dissolved*. New York: Basic Books, 1978.

Cohen, Bernard, "Political Communication on the Japanese Peace Settlement." In *American Political Interest Groups: Readings in Theory and Research*. edited by Betty H. Zisk, pp. 226–37. Belmont, California: Wadsworth Publishing Co., 1969.

Cox, Archibald. *The Role of the Supreme Court in American Government*. New York: Oxford University Press, 1976.

Davis, Kenneth C. *Administrative Law,* 6th ed. St Paul, Minnesota: West Publishing, 1977.

————. *Administrative Law of the Seventies*. Rochester, New York: Lawyers Co-operative Publishing Co., 1976.

————. *Administrative Law Text,* 3rd ed. St. Paul, Minnesota: West Publishing, 1972.

————. *Administrative Law Treatise,* 2d ed. vol. 1. San Diego, California: University of California, 1978.

Donnelly, Warren H. *Effect of Calvert Cliffs and Other Court Decisions Upon Nuclear Power in the United States*. U.S. Congress, Senate. Serial No. 92-28. Washington, D.C.: United States Government Printing Office, 1972.

Ebbin, Steve and Kasper, Raphael. *Citizen Groups and the Nuclear Power Controversy: Uses of Scientific and Technical Information*. Cambridge, Massachusetts: MIT Press, 1974.

Edison Electric Institute. *Edison Electric Institute Statistical Yearbook of the Electric Utility Industry for 1977*. New York: Edison Electric Institute, October, 1978.

Liroff, Richard A. *A National Policy for the Environment: NEPA and Its Aftermath,* Bloomington, Indiana: Indiana University Press, 1976.

Murphy, Arthur W. *The Nuclear Power Controversy*. Englewood Cliffs, New Jersey: Prentice-Hall, 1976.

Nader, Ralph and Abbotts, John. *The Menace of Atomic Energy*. New York: W.W. Norton and Co., 1977.

Novick, Sheldon. *The Electric War: The Fight Over Nuclear Power*. San Francisco: Sierra Club Books, 1976.

Peltason, Jack. *Federal Courts in the Political Process*. New York: Random House, 1955.

Rohde, David and Spaeth, Harold. *Supreme Court Decision Making*. San Francisco: W.H. Freeman, 1976.

Sax, Joseph. *Defending the Environment*. New York: Alfred Knopf, 1971.

Schattschneider, E.E. *Politics, Pressures and the Tariff*. New York: Prentice-Hall, 1935.

Schubert, Glendon. *Judicial Policy-Making: The Political Role of the Courts*. Chicago: Scott, Foresman, 1965.

Schumacher, E.F. *Small Is Beautiful*. New York: Harper and Row, 1975.

Scigliano, Robert. *The Supreme Court and the Presidency*. New York: Free Press, 1971.

Shapiro, Martin. *The Supreme Court and Administrative Agencies*. New York: Free Press, 1968.

Smith, David Horton and Baldwin, Burt R. "Voluntary Associations and Volunteering in the United States." In *Voluntary Action Research: 1974*. Edited by David Horton Smith. Lexington, Mass.: Lexington Books, 1974. Cited in Jeffrey M. Berry, *Lobbying for the People*, p. 287. Princeton, N.J.: Princeton University Press, 1977.

Truman, David. *The Governmental Process*. New York: Alfred Knopf, 1960.

U.S. Atomic Energy Commission, WASH-1174. *The Nuclear Industry 1974*. Washington, D.C., 1975. In Ralph Nader and John Abbotts, *The Menace of Atomic Energy*, p. 265. New York: W.W. Norton and Co., 1977.

Vose, Clement. *Caucasians Only: The Supreme Court, the NAACP, and the Restrictive Covenant Cases*. Berkeley: University of California Press, 1959.

Wasby, Stephen L. *The Impact of the United States Supreme Court*. Homewood, Illinois: The Dorsey Press, 1970.

Periodicals

Albert, Lee A. "Standing to Challenge Administrative Action." *Yale Law Journal* 83 (January, 1974):425–497.

Bazelon, David. "Coping with Technology through the Legal Process." *Cornell Law Review* 62 (June, 1977):817–832.

———. "The Impact of the Courts on Public Administration." *Indiana Law Journal* 52 (Fall, 1976):101–110.

Berlin, Edward; Roisman, Anthony; and Kessler, Gladys. "Public Interest Law." *George Washington Law Review* 38 (May, 1970):675–693.

Breitkopf, Laurel. "The National Environmental Policy Act of 1969 and Nuclear Power Plant Licensing." *DePaul Law Review* 26 (Spring, 1977):666–681.

Claggett, B.M. "Informal Action—Adjudication—Rulemaking." *Duke Law Journal* (1971):51–58.

Dupont, Norman. "Judicial Review of Generic Rulemaking." *Georgetown Law Journal* 65 (June, 1977):1295–1323.

"Environmental Law: Public Participation in the Environmental Impact Statement Process." *Minnesota Law Review* 61 (January, 1977): 363–381.

"EPRI Finds Nuclear Cheaper on Average." *Nuclear News* 20 (December, 1977):35.

Fawkes, Lee Bohn, "Environmental Law—Nuclear Power Plants." *Annual Survey of American Law* (1976):587–609.

Gardner, Warren and Greensberger, I. Michael. "Judicial Review of Administrative Action and Responsible Government." *Georgetown Law Journal* 63 (October, 1974):7–38.

Gendlin, Frances. "The Palisades Protest: A Pattern of Citizen Intervention." *Science and Public Affairs* 27 (November, 1971):53–56.

Graham, Frank, Jr. "The Outrageous Mr. Cherry and the Underachieving Nukes." *Audubon* 79 (September, 1977):50–67.

Grainey, Michael W. "Nuclear Reactor Regulation." *Gonzaga Law Review* 11 (Spring, 1976):809–837.

Hamilton, Robert. "Procedures for the Adoption of Rules of General Applicability: The Need for Procedural Innovation in Administrative Rulemaking." *California Law Review* 60 (1972):1276–1337.

Hohenemser, Kurt H.; Kasperson, Roger; and Kates, Robert. "The Distrust of Nuclear Power." *Science* 196 (April 1, 1977):25–34.

Howard, J.W. "Litigation Flow in Three U.S. Courts of Appeals." *Law and Society Review* 8 (Fall, 1973):33–53.

"Implementing the National Environmental Policy Act through Rulemaking: The Implications of NRDC v. NRC." *University of Pennsylvania Law Review* 126 (November, 1977):148–203.

Jaffe, Louis L. "Standing Again." *Harvard Law Review* 84 (January, 1971):633–38.

Keating, William Thomas. "Politics, Energy and the Environment." *American Behavioral Scientist* 19 (September/October, 1975):37–74.

"Labor Would Accelerate Use of Coal, Nuclear." *Nuclear News* 20 (April, 1977):54.

Lamb, Charles. "Exploring the Conservatism of Federal Appeals Court Judges." *Indiana Law Journal* 51 (Winter, 1976):257-79.

Like, Irving. "Multi-Media Confrontation—The Environmentalists' Strategy for a 'No-Win' Agency Proceeding." *Atomic Energy Law Journal* 13 (Spring, 1971):1.

McGarry, J. Michael III and Conner, Troy B., Jr. "Nuclear Alternative: An Analysis of Paralysis." *Hastings Law Journal* 28 (May, 1977): 1209-1243.

Monaghan, Henry P. "Constitutional Adjudication: The Who and When." *Yale Law Review* 82 (June, 1973):1363-1397.

Murphy, Arthur W. "The National Environmental Policy Act and the Licensing Process: Environmentalist Magna Carta or Agency Coup de Grace." *Columbia Law Review* 72 (October, 1972):963-1007.

Murphy, Arthur W. and La Pierre, D. Bruce. "Nuclear 'Moratorium' Legislation in the States and the Supremacy Clause: A Case of Express Preemption." *Columbia Law Review* 76 (April, 1976):392-456.

"Nuclear News Briefs." *Nuclear News* 20 (February, 1977):17.

Orren, Karen. "Standing to Sue: Interest Group Conflict in the Federal Courts." *American Political Science Review* 70 (September, 1976): 723-741.

Paglin, Max D. and Shor, Edgar. "Regulatory Agency Responses to the Development of Public Participation." *Public Administration Review* (March/April, 1977):140-48.

Palfrey, John Gorham. "Energy and the Environment: The Special Case of Nuclear Power." *Columbia Law Review* 74 (December, 1974):1375-1409.

Poulin, Joyce Wheeler. "Who Controls Low-Level Radioactive Wastes?" *Environmental Affairs* 6 (1977):201-25.

Robie, Ronald B. "Recognition of Substantive Rights Under NEPA." *Natural Resources Lawyer* VII (Summer, 1974):387-438.

Roisman, Anthony Z. "Suing for Safety." *Trial* 10 (January-February, 1974):13-16.

Schuck, Peter H. "Public Interest Groups and the Policy Process." *Public Administration Review* 37 (March/April, 1977):132-40.

Scott, Kenneth. "Standing in the Supreme Court." *Harvard Law Review* 86 (February, 1973):645-92.

Sedler, Robert A. "Standing Justiciability, and All That: A Behavioral Analysis." *Vanderbilt Law Review* 25 (April, 1972):479-512.

"Slaying the Nuclear Giants: Is California's New Nuclear Power Plant Siting Legislation Shielded Against the Attack of Federal Preemption?" *Pacific Law Journal* 8 (July, 1977):741-82.

Smith, Don S. And Lancaster, A. Angela. "Nuclear Power's Effects on Electric Rate Making." *Public Utilities Fortnightly* 101 (February 2, 1978):16–22.

Stern, Robert. "The Solicitor General's Office and Administrative Agency Litigation." *American Bar Association Journal* 46 (February, 1960): 154–218.

"Survey of the Governmental Regulation of Nuclear Power Generation." *Marquette Law Review* 59 (1976):836–855.

"The Judicial Role in Defining Procedural Requirements for Agency Rule-making." *Howard Law Review* 87 (1974):782–806.

"Three Thousand Pronuclears Hold Manchester Rally." *Nuclear News* 20 (August, 1977):50.

Tucker, William. "Environmentalism and the Leisure Class." *Harper's* 225 (December, 1977):49–80.

Verkuil, Paul. "Judicial Review of Informal Rulemaking." *Virginia Law Review* 60 (1974):185–249.

Vose, Clement. "Litigation As a Form of Pressure Group Activity." *Annals of the American Academy of Political and Social Science* 319 (September, 1958):20–31.

"Washington and the Utilities." *Public Utilities Fortnightly* 101 (April 13, 1978):35.

Williams, Stephen. "'Hybrid Rulemaking' under the Administrative Procedure Act." *University of Chicago Law Review* 42 (1975):401–456.

Wright, Skelly. "Court of Appeals Review of Federal Regulatory Agency Rulemaking." *Administrative Law Review* 26 (1974):199–212.

———. "The Courts and the Rulemaking Process: The Limits of Judicial Review." *Cornell Law Review* 59 (1974):375–397.

Yellin, Joel. "Judicial Review and Nuclear Power: Assessing the Risks of Environmental Catastrophe." *George Washington Law Review* 45 (August, 1977):969–993.

Newspapers and Newsletters

Anderson, Jack and Whitten, Les. "Atomic Watergate Operation." Syndicated Column, 11 August 1977.

———. "Nuclear Industry Blasts TV Networks." *Detroit Free Press,* 26 June 1977, p. 3C.

"A Siege at Seabrook." *The Free Paper,* Boston, Massachusetts, 14 May 1977, p. 1.

Burnham, David. "G.E. Warns of Halt in Making Reactors." *The New York Times,* 15 May 1977, p. 1.

"Carter's Lawyer Calls Own Shots." *Detroit Free Press,* 29 December 1977, p. 1B.

Charlton, Linda. "Ralph Nader's Conglomerate Is Big Business." *New York Times,* 29 January 1978, p. 3.

"Clergymen Rip Midland Nuclear Plants." *Detroit News,* 30 April 1978, p. 25B.

Cowan, Edward. "Schlesinger Urges Conserving Energy." *The New York Times,* 24 December 1976, p. A11.

Dickey, Sandra L. "N-Plant Legal Fight Nearly Over." *Saginaw News,* 4 April 1978, p. 1.

"Dow Hits Tactics of Nuclear Foes." *Midland Daily News,* 18 January 1971, p. 1.

"Dow Seeks Early N-Hearing." *Midland Daily News,* 2 August 1971, p. 1.

Emschwiller, John R. "Nuclear Nemesis: Using the Law's Delay, Myron Cherry Attacks Atomic Power Projects." *The Wall Street Journal,* 10 March 1978, p. 1.

"Final Questions Must End 'N' Plant Delay." Editorial, *Midland Daily News,* 13 April 1971, p. 4.

"Firm Will Cut Radioactive Waste at Plant." *Midland Daily News,* 29 March 1971, p. 1.

Garrett, Fred E. "Attorney's Lawsuit 'a Terrible Tangle'." *Saginaw News,* 25 January 1978, p. B4.

———. "Suit Reflects Nuclear 'Fallout'." *Saginaw News,* 29 January 1978, p. G1.

Golden, William P. "Wives Will Rejoice in Midland A-Plant." *Jackson Citizen Patriot,* 17 December 1967, p. 1.

Herring, Betty. "McConnell Says No Need for Fear Over N-Plant." *Midland Daily News,* 22 October 1970, p. 1.

Hill, Gladwyn. "California's Case Study in Nuclear Politics." *The New York Times,* 5 March 1978, p. E3.

"In Nuclear-Powered Bind." Editorial, *Bay City Times,* 7 December 1969, p. 4.

Jasen, Georgette. "In the Fight Over Nuclear Energy's Role, Friends and Foes Are Deeply Committed." *The Wall Street Journal,* 21 July 1977, p. 26.

"Liberal Activists Generally Praise their Colleagues Serving Carter." *The Wall Street Journal,* 6 January 1978, p. 1.

McGee, Gay. "Midland Housewife Initiated Nuclear Plant Hassle." *Bay City Times,* 6 June 1971, p. C1.

"N-Hearing Zeroes in on Birds, Fish, and Trees." *Bay City Times,* 30 May 1972, p. 3A.

"N-Plant Backers Refute Claims by Mrs. Sinclair." *Midland Daily News,* 23 August 1971, p. 1.

"N-Plant Construction Delayed Pending OK." *Midland Daily News,* 14 November 1970, p. 1.

"N-Plant Endorsed by Five Labor Unions." *Midland Daily News,* 5 October 1971, p. 1.

"Nuclear Plant Lag Rapped by Utility." *Jackson Citizen Patriot,* 1 November 1978, p. 1.

Nucleonics Week 18 (13 January 1977):9.

Nucleonics Week 18 (5 May 1977):16.

Nucleonics Week 18 (6 October 1977):11.

Nucleonics Week 18 (15 December 1977):10.

Nucleonics Week 19 (30 March 1978):4.

Nucleonics Week 19 (18 May 1978):9-10.

Nucleonics Week 19 (28 September 1978):11.

Nucleonics Week 20 (10 May 1979):10.

O'Connor, John. "High Court Hearing Is Expensive." *Jackson Citizen Patriot,* 29 May 1978, p. 4.

Peterson, John E. "Energy Plan Dooms Poor, NAACP Says." *Detroit News,* 8 January 1978, p. 1.

Petition for Leave to Intervene (State of Kansas). Quoted in "Kansas Likely to Enter Midland N-Plant Case." *Midland Daily News,* 18 September 1971, p. 1.

Plastrik, Pete. "Nuclear Safety Spurs State Action." *Jackson Citizen Patriot,* 6 June 1978, p. 3.

Puravs, John A. "We Got More Heat Than Light." *Saginaw News,* 25 April 1978, p. A7.

Rathje, Kenneth, Chairman of the Saginaw UAW Community Action Program Council. "Letter to the Editor." *Midland Daily News,* 20 August 1971, p. 4.

Schneider, Phillip L. "Motion to Dismiss Mapleton Intervenors on Tap Monday." *Midland Daily News,* 20 May 1972, p. 1.

"Shutdown of Midland Sought During Rally for Nuclear Plant." *Midland Daily News,* 30 September 1971, p. 1.

Sinclair, Mary. "Historic Case Will Test AEC Powers, Standards, and Licensing Practices." *Essexville-Hampton Observer,* 19 November 1970, p. 1.

"Small Step Forward in Power Controversy." Editorial, *Midland Daily News,* 18 March 1971, p. 4.

Smith, Roger. "Stabilizing Nuclear Licensing Requirements Essential, Says AIF Report." *Nucleonics Week* 19 (January 26, 1978):1.

———. "The Next Three Years Look Terrible for Nuclear Power." *Nucleonics Week* 18 (November 24, 1977):1-2.

———. "Utilities Would Buy Nuclear—If Only Carter Speaks Out, Industry Feels." *Nucleonics Week* 20 (29 March 1979):2-3.

Steketee, Peter, Chairman of the West Michigan Environmental Action Council. "Letter to the Editor." *Midland Daily News,* 26 April 1971, p. 4.

Stevens, Lynn. "NRC Attorneys Trying to Ban Myron Cherry from All Licensing Proceedings." *Nucleonics Week* 19 (5 January 1978):3.

"Supreme Court Defines Narrower Role for Courts in Nuclear Field." *Nucleonics Week* 19 (6 April 1978):3-4.

Weaver, Warren Jr. "Burger Court is Limiting Its Own Turf." *The New York Times,* 9 April 1978, p. E2.

———. "Inevitably the Environment Has Gone to Court." *The New York Times,* 30 October 1977, p. E2.

Organizational Publications with a Limited Circulation

American Assembly, *Report on Nuclear Energy,* April 22-25, 1976.

Atomic Industrial Forum. *INFO* 98, September, 1976 and January, 1978.

———. "1978 Economic Survey Results," 14 May 1979.

———. "Profile of U.S. Nuclear Power Development," 31 December 1978.

———. "The California Initiative," 9 June 1976.

Consumers Power Company. "Chronology of Project Cost Revisions." Jackson, Michigan, 1976.

———. "Important Progress Dates: Midland Nuclear Plant." Jackson, Michigan.

———. *Inside,* 16 December 1977.

———. Press Release, 3 April 1978.

Edison Electric Institute, 1978 Public Information Research Program. *The Electric Utility Industry Today.* New York: Edison Electric Institute, 1978.

Fiorino, Daniel. "The Federal Courts and the Regulatory Process: The Cases of Natural Gas and Broadcasting." Ph.D. diss., The Johns Hopkins University, 1977.

United States Atomic Energy Commission. *Exceptions of the Intervenors before the Atomic Safety and Licensing Appeals Board.* 15 January 1973.

Westinghouse Electric Corporation. *Resources: Nuclear Energy Information.*

Legal Briefs and Documents

Case of Nelson Aeschliman v. United States Nuclear Regulatory Commission:

Brief for Petitioners, Saginaw Valley Nuclear Study Group et al. and Nelson Aeschliman et al., and Reply briefs.

Brief for Respondents, U.S. Nuclear Regulatory Commission, et al.

Brief for Intervenor, Consumers Power Company.

General Docket for N. Aeschliman v. USNRC and NRDC v. USNRC, provided by the Clerk, U.S. Court of Appeals for the District of Columbia Circuit.

Cases of Vermont Yankee Nuclear Power Corporation v. Natural Resources Defense Council, Inc. et al. and Consumers Power Company v. Aeschliman, et al.:

Brief for Petitioner, Vermont Yankee Nuclear Power Corporation.

Brief for Petitioner, Consumers Power Company, and Reply brief.

Brief for Respondents, Natural Resources Defense Council, Inc. et al.

Brief for Respondents, Saginaw Valley Nuclear Study Group, et al.

Brief for Respondents, Baltimore Gas and Electric Company, et al.

Brief for the Federal Respondents, Solicitor General and the NRC.

Brief for Amici Curiae, Hans A. Bethe, et al., Members of Scientists and Engineers for Secure Energy and Mid–America Legal Foundation.

Brief for Amici Curiae, Edison Electric Institute, et al.

Brief for Amicus Curiae, U.S. Labor Party.

Brief for Amicus Curiae, Union of Concerned Scientists Fund, Inc.

Brief for Amici Curiae, 24 Named States.

Addresses

Carter, Jimmy. "Nuclear Energy and World Order." United Nations, 13 May 1976.

Georgine, Robert, AFL–CIO. Edison Electric Institute, 45th Annual Convention, 14 June 1977.

Kristol, Irving, American Enterprise Institute. Edison Electric Institute, 45th Annual Convention, 13 June 1977.

Lewis, Floyd, Chairman of Edison Electric Institute. Edison Electric Institute, 45th Annual Convention, 13 June 1977.

Rustin, Bayard, A. Philip Randolph Institute. Edison Electric Institute, 45th Annual Convention, 14 June 1977.

Theberge, Leonard J., President, National Legal Center for the Public Interest. Atomic Industrial Forum, 23 February 1978.

Vogel, David. "Promoting Pluralism: The Public Interest Movement and the American Reform Tradition." Paper delivered at the annual meeting of the American Political Science Association, New York, New York, September, 1978.

Interviews

Bacon, Judd. Managing Attorney, Consumers Power Company, Jackson, Michigan. Interview, 19 September 1978; telephone interview, 8 June 1979.

Conner, Roger. Leader, West Michigan Environmental Action Council, Grand Rapids, Michigan. Telephone interview, 19 October 1978.

Coy, Roderick S. Assistant Attorney General for the State of Michigan, Lansing, Michigan. Telephone interview, 25 October 1979.

Jensen, Roland. Director of Corporate Strategic Planning, Northern States Power Company, Minneapolis, Minnesota. Interview, 14 May 1978.

Luria, Daniel. Research Department, United Auto Workers, Detroit, Michigan. Telephone interview, 18 October 1978.

Marshall, Wendall. Leader, Mapleton Intervenors, Mapleton, Michigan. Telephone interview, 18 October 1978.

Sax, Joseph. Professor of Law, University of Michigan, Ann Arbor, Michigan. Interview, 3 October 1978.

Sinclair, Mary. Leader, Saginaw Valley Nuclear Study Group, Midland, Michigan. Interview, 11 October 1978.

Theberge, Leonard J. President, National Legal Center for the Public Interest, Washington, D.C. Interview, 17 May 1978.

Vining, Joseph. Professor of Law, University of Michigan, Ann Arbor, Michigan. Interview, 6 February 1979.

Index

About the Author

Constance Ewing Cook attended both Wellesley and Barnard colleges, graduating from Barnard in 1964. She subsequently received the masters degree from The Pennsylvania State University and received the doctorate in political science from Boston University in 1979. She has taught at Northeastern University (University College) in Boston, and is currently teaching political science at Albion College in Albion, Michigan.